Thinking English

Thinking English

A new intermediate course

Michael Thorn

Cassell · London

CASSELL LTD
1 St Anne's Road
Eastbourne, East Sussex, BN21 3UN

First published 1982

ISBN 0 304 30625 8

Illustrations by Rodney Paull

Designed by Jacky Wedgwood

Phototypesetting by Georgia Origination, Liverpool

Printed and bound in Hungary

Grateful acknowledgement for permission to use photographs
reproduced in this book is made to the following (numbers refer
to the pages in book on which they occur).

M. Arora (133R); Barnaby's Picture Library (33B, 46, 102, 121,
140T); Barry Lewis/Network Photographers (55); BBC Hulton
Picture Library (75T, 98, 105, 129); Cadbury Schweppes Ltd
(26); Camera Press (60); Hamleys Ltd (59), Keystone Press
Agency (17, 71, 75BL, 89); Mayflower Studio (111); Moss Bros
Ltd (133L); Popperfoto (42, 85, 139R, 140B); John Redman
(117, photo shows George Daniels); Rex Features (75BR, 78);
Rolls Royce Motors Ltd (49); *The Times* (23); Michael Thorn
(10, 29, 33M and B, 36, 62, 73, 86, 123, 139L); Trusthouse
Forte Catering Ltd (62); Victoria and Albert Museum (68)

Contents

To the student

Thinking English is the fourth volume in the Cassell Foundation English Course, so if you are studying this book, you will already have worked through *Exploring English* or some similar intermediate course book.

By now your knowledge of English grammar and structures must be pretty good. You should now be able to write accurately in English, but you probably want to write in different styles and express yourself. In order to do this, you will need to enlarge your vocabulary and feel confident about your use of structures.

In this book you will find reading texts that are more demanding than any you have studied before. We hope they will interest you, help you to widen your vocabulary and lead to interesting discussions.

We have provided plenty of short practice exercises, designed to reinforce your knowledge of basic structures and sometimes to help you to express ideas in a more sophisticated way.

The taped listening material gives you a chance to listen to native speakers expressing their opinions and feelings in dialogues and in speeches. The practice activities will make you even more conscious of the importance of how things are said, and you will be able to practise, using the examples we have suggested.

Phrasal verbs are a constant worry for students learning English and you will find that we have introduced these gradually, unit by unit, so that by the time you finish the book, you will have met all of the most common ones and will feel confident when using them.

Being able to speak languages other than your own can open all sorts of doors and make life more fun. Perhaps English is the nearest thing we have to a world language. We hope this book will help you to improve your English and that you will enjoy using it. It could not have been written without Joanna Gray's contributions and Joy McKellen's very valuable editorial help.

London 1982   Michael Thorn

UNIT 1   The family

Reading activity

THE ONLY CHILD?

1   I was one of six children. I have two younger brothers and three elder sisters.
My father was not a wealthy man and we lived in a three-bedroomed house, so
conditions at home were always quite cramped and there was little privacy.
Yet I consider that I was extremely fortunate. The house was on the outskirts
5   of a small town. Meadows, woods and even a friendly stream lay within
walking distance of our home. My mother and father were far too busy to
occupy themselves with my affairs, so the greater part of my upbringing was
left to my sisters. If I am now a comparatively calm and placid person, able to
cope tolerably well with those problems that life invariably presents us with, it
10   is, I firmly believe, due to the fact that I was allowed to grow up without too
much fuss being made of me.

The most dreadful fate that I can imagine would be that of growing up as an
only child. All mothers and fathers experiment on their unfortunate first-
born. They read the latest baby books, they attend clinics and courses of
15   lectures. They listen to the advice of maiden aunts. They distress themselves
over the little person's digestion. They debate the exact moment to present
him or her with solid food. What they find extremely difficult to do is to allow
their child to grow up at his own pace, to make his own mistakes and quietly
learn from them.

20   As soon as the second baby is on the way, the first escapes from this period of
close attention. He begins to get away with things. He discovers that even if he
does eat sandwiches with dirty hands, or unripe apples that have fallen from

the tree, he is not invariably sick in the night. He acquires a sense of proportion regarding his own importance.

25 But what happens to the only child? Never, or at least not until it is far too late to do anything about it, does he or she escape from the minute examination of his every action. It is a miracle if he does not grow up a nervous wreck, a hypochondriac constantly worrying about his health, a wholly self-centred being, who shivers at the sight of his own reflection in the mirror.

A Questions

1 Do you think the writer had a room of his own? What is the reason for your answer?
2 What does the writer mean by 'a friendly stream'? (line 5)
3 What sort of things do you think the writer's big sisters did for him?
4 Do you think the writer is a nervous sort of person? What is the reason for your answer?
5 What does the writer think a child should be allowed to do?
6 Can you explain why it might be difficult for an only child to do this?
7 What kind of things is a child able to do after a new baby is born?
8 What do you think a hypochondriac is? (line 28)

B Vocabulary exercise

1 Think of some different ways of becoming *wealthy*.
2 Somebody once said: 'The one important thing that money can buy is *privacy*'. What did he mean by this?
3 The writer claims to have a *calm* and *placid* temperament. When might this be useful? What words might we use to describe the opposite sort of temperament?
4 The writer speaks of *coping with problems*. What kind of problems would you have to cope with on a week's camping holiday?
5 Doctors are *experimenting* all the time to find cures for illnesses. Name some of these illnesses.
6 Children often try to *get away with* not doing things like washing their hands. What do you remember trying to get away with when you were young?
7 Who might carry out a *minute* examination of what?
8 When do people usually *shiver*?

C Vocabulary exercise

It is very important to understand how words can change their meanings in different contexts. In the writer's story of his own family, 'The only child?', he says: 'They present him or her with *solid* food.' (line 17) The word 'solid' has different meanings. Here are some: heavy; dependable; strong; not liquid. Look at this example and choose the right definition for the word as it is used in the passage.

Example: They present him with *solid* food.
   a heavy
   b dependable
   c strong
   d not liquid

You should read the second paragraph again and remember who 'they' are and who 'him or her' are. Then discuss your answer with a neighbour.

Here are more dictionary definitions of words and phrases used in the Reading activity. Choose the right definition for the word as it is used in the passage.

1 *Conditions* at home were always cramped. (line 3)
   a circumstances
   b provisions
   c social positions
   d facilities

2 Yet I *consider* that I was extremely fortunate. (line 4)
   a think about
   b believe
   c regard
   d think of

3 My mother and father were far too busy to *occupy themselves with* my affairs. (line 6)
   a take up
   b live in
   c hold
   d concentrate on

4 They *attend* clinics and courses of lectures.
(line 14)

   a look after   **c** go with

   b go to   **d** listen to

5 As soon as the second baby is on the way, the
first *escapes from* this period of close attention.
(line 20)

   a avoids   **c** is forgotten by

   b gets away with   **d** gets away from

D   Discussion

Find out if there is anyone in your class who has no
brothers or sisters. Is there anyone who has more
than one brother or sister? Do you think the writer
is right when he says it must be awful to be an only
child?

Did you ever have to look after younger brothers or
sisters? What did you think about it?

If money were no problem, what do you think
would be the ideal number of children?

What differences would you like to see in their
ages?

E   Practice activity

Study these sentences:

All mothers and fathers *experiment* on their
unfortunate first-born. (line 13) They *read* the latest
baby books. (line 14)

The verbs in these sentences are in the *simple
present*. They tell us about things the parents
always do, or usually do.

Can you find *eight* more verbs like this in the text?
Underline the verbs.

Note this sentence:
It is a miracle if he does not grow up a nervous
wreck. (line 27)

We form the negative of the *simple present* with 'do
not' and 'does not'.

I like green apples, but my brother *doesn't*. I *don't*
usually *go* to work by car, I walk.

Kate, Peter, Jane, Tom and Angela are all getting
married soon. They have agreed to answer some
questions for a magazine article. (See table below.)

Now you answer these questions:

1 How does Kate feel about cooking?

2 How does Angela feel about cooking?

3 What is Jane's opinion about girls working
after they're married?

4 What is Tom's opinion about girls working
after they're married?

5 How does Tom feel about divorce?

6 How does Jane feel about divorce?

7 What does Peter think about money?

8 What does Angela think about money?

9 What do most of them feel about men wearing
a wedding ring?

	Kate	Peter	Jane	Tom	Angela
Do you enjoy cooking?	Yes	No	Yes	Yes	No
Do you think it's a good idea for women to continue to work after they are married?	Yes	Yes	Yes	No	Yes
Do you believe that divorce is too easy in England today?	No	No	No	Yes	No
Do you think money is important?	Yes	Yes	Yes	Yes	No
Do you think that men should wear a wedding ring as well as women?	Yes	Yes	Yes	No	Yes

F   Practice activity

The following adjectives and adverbs were used in the text:

busy, cramped, comparatively, difficult, dirty, dreadful, extremely, firmly, invariably, latest, placid, quietly, quite, small, unfortunate, unripe.

Use *some* of these words to fill the gaps in the text below. Each word may be used once only:

My father was an _____ quiet man, while my mother was small, energetic and talkative. At the end of the garden there was a _____ shed which my father called his workshop. He had an _____ habit of disappearing there just before mealtimes with the _____ copy of the 'Do-it-yourself' magazine and I would _____ be sent to fetch him. Conditions in the workshop were very _____, for that was where the lawn-mower lived, as well as all the garden tools, two bicycles and a _____ old washing machine that needed a new motor. 'I'll be along in a moment', he would say, 'I'm _____ just now', so my mother would place his dinner on the table and by the time he came in it would be _____ cold. He would grumble _____ and my mother would tell him, pleasantly but _____, that she wasn't running a hotel and that he should come when he was called.

G   Practice activity

Study this sentence:
He discovers that even if he *does* eat sandwiches with dirty hands . . . he is not invariably sick in the night. (line 21)

We could express this idea without 'does':
. . . even if he eats sandwiches with dirty hands . . .
But by stressing 'does', the writer makes his point more effectively.

Look at the sentences below. Practise saying them with stress on the words in *italics* and discuss how the meaning changes according to where the stress falls.

1   I *do* hope you can come to the party on Saturday.
2   I hope you *can* come to the party on Saturday.
3   *I* hope you can come to the party.
4   I *am* sorry you can't come to the party.
5   I'm sorry *you* can't come to the party.
6   *I'm* sorry you can't come to the party.
7   Thank you, I *did* enjoy the party.
8   Oh yes, *I* enjoyed the party.

H   Practice activity

Note this sentence from the Reading activity:

He begins to *get away with* things. (line 21)

The verb 'get' is frequently used with prepositions and adverbs:

Peter *gets about* a lot. Last month he was in Vienna and tomorrow he's off to Moscow.
Did you *get back* the gloves you lost?
When she *got off* the camel, she was shaking like a leaf.
'*Get out of* here', he shouted.
Little girls usually find it easier to *get round* their fathers than their mothers.
It took her a long time to *get over* the death of her husband.
He *got through* the exam at the second attempt.
The thief *got in* through the bathroom window.
Why did you *get up* so early this morning?

Replace the words in italics by suitable expressions with 'get'. Use each expression once only.
1   *Leave* this house immediately.
2   The police *entered* through the back door.
3   He *rose* early and walked down to the lake.
4   He never really *recovered* from the shock.
5   Did you *pass* your test?
6   She *recovered* her purse but there was no money in it.
7   The jockey *dismounted* and looked anxiously at one of his horse's front legs.
8   My uncle *travels* a great deal.

UNIT 1 The family

Dialogue 🔊

Tony and Richard are both students at Prestham Polytechnic. They are sharing digs, although their ages and backgrounds are very different.

Before you listen to their conversation, you will need to *study* the impression questions. While you listen, you should *think about* the impression questions. After you have listened, you can *discuss* your impressions.

I Impression questions

1 Who do you think is more mature, Tony or Richard? Can you use at least two adjectives to support your opinion?
2 Why do you think Tony is asking so many questions?
3 What words would you use to describe the sort of person Richard seems to be?
4 How would you describe Richard's relationship with his brother?
5 What differences do you notice in Richard's answers as the conversation continues?
6 Why do you think Richard's answers are different?

J Focus questions

In the dialogue there are several examples of incomplete questions. For example, Richard says 'Name?' If he were speaking formally or to a stranger, he would ask the full question: 'What is his name?' Now write the full questions for these incomplete questions.

1 'Older or younger?'
2 'How much?'
3 'Get on all right?'

Now decide whether your voice should rise or fall when you ask these questions and mark the last word in the question with an arrow, like this ↗ or ↘. Then compare your answers with a neighbour and decide why the intonation is different.

K Focus questions

There are also several examples of stress used to emphasise the speaker's meaning. For example, Richard says, 'When I have a *real* problem, I discuss it with Mark.' Richard stresses 'real' because he wants to emphasise that he is not talking about an ordinary problem. Now look at these examples from the dialogue. Underline the words you think should be stressed.

RICHARD   When I have a real problem, I discuss it with Mark.

TONY   And what is a real problem?

RICHARD   Money is one.

TONY   You say money is one problem.

RICHARD   Of course there are. He knows who my friends are and I know who his friends are.

Listen to the dialogue again and change your answers if necessary. After you have done this, explain what special meaning the speaker wants to emphasise.

L Focus questions

Here are more examples of conversations where stress is used to show meaning. Underline the word you think should be stressed in the *answers*.

TONY   I've found the answer to that exam question.
RICHARD   Really? What is the answer?

RICHARD   Did you answer both questions correctly?
TONY   Well, I answered one.

TONY   Do you know that girl over there?
RICHARD   Well, I know who she is.

TONY   Have you met our landlady's husband?
RICHARD   No, but I've met her sister.

TONY   Do you know who left the lights on last night?
RICHARD   I know I didn't.

When you have checked that your answers are right, practise saying the questions and answers with a neighbour.

The family

Listening activity 📼

M Comprehension

Here are seven statements referring to the interview. Decide whether they are true or false:

1 Professor Taylor has written several books.
2 Professor Taylor says that in Britain 40 years ago it was normal for a widowed mother to go and live with one of her married children.
3 The interviewer suggests that it might be a help to a young married woman to have her mother living with her.
4 The old people are usually keen to go and live with their married sons or daughters.
5 Life expectancy is increasing because the birth-rate has fallen.
6 Private nursing homes are dreadfully expensive.
7 The Professor says that a lot of money is going to be spent on providing more homes for the elderly.

N Gap dictation

Here is part of the interview between Professor Taylor and Norman Blunt, with certain words missing. Listen to the interview again and write in the missing words.

PROF. TAYLOR   . . . as long as old people are able to (1)_____ themselves, the system works quite well. But (2)_____ they need (3)_____ in the way of care and attention, the situation becomes very difficult indeed.

NORMAN BLUNT   Well, presumably a point comes when old people (4)_____ into a nursing home or (5)_____.

PROF. TAYLOR   Yes, but it's not (6)_____. Because of improvements in medical science, life expectancy is increasing (7)_____. The birth-rate has fallen. This means that an ever smaller working population is having to (8)_____ an ever larger number of old people, (9)_____ care and attention. The number of places in old people's homes provided by the State is strictly limited. There *are* private nursing homes, but the cost is (10)_____ of the average family.

O Writing activity

Listen to the interview again and take notes. Answer these questions, then summarise the Professor's arguments.

1 Does the Professor think old people are a problem? Why?
2 What does he say about young married couples and parents living together?
3 What are the problems with State nursing homes and private nursing homes?
4 What should be done? Why is it difficult to do this?

P Writing activity

Professor Taylor paints a rather sad picture of grandparents in Britain, doesn't he? Describe the situation in your country. Write one paragraph of 120–150 words.

15

Summary

In this unit we revise the *simple present* tense.

Examples:
I never get up before eight o'clock.
He always goes to work by train.

Remember the question form:
When *do you* get up?
Why *does he* go by train?

We also use 'do' and 'does' with the negative:
I *don't believe* in divorce.
He *doesn't wear* a wedding ring.

Explain why the *simple present* is used in the examples above.

We also practise using adverbs and adjectives:

Examples of adjectives:
It was a *difficult* decision.
She was *happy* while she was there.
They were *friendly* people.

Examples of adverbs:
It was a *comparatively* difficult decision to make.
She was *very* happy while she was there.
I think he behaved *generously* in the circumstances.

When do we use adverbs and when do we use adjectives?

Note too how we can change the meaning of a sentence by changing the stress on individual words.
For example: 'I *paid* the bill' is simply an assurance that the bill has been paid. However, '*I* paid the bill' *might* be said in rather a nasty tone.

Finally note that 'get' is often used as a phrasal verb: to get about, to get back, to get off, to get out, to get round, to get over, to get through, to get in and to get up.

Give an example of something we might *get off* and something we might *get over*.

UNIT 2　　Pop music

Reading activity

THE BEATLES

1　When John Lennon was murdered outside his New York apartment by a
　　young man for whom he had earlier autographed a record sleeve, it signalled
　　the end of an era. The faint hope that one day the Beatles might get together
　　again had gone for ever.

5　The Beatles: George Harrison, John Lennon, Paul McCartney and Ringo
　　Starr, were formed in Liverpool in 1960. Harrison, Lennon and McCartney
　　had gained experience playing at a club in Hamburg, but it was at the
　　'Cavern', in Liverpool, their home city, that the Beatles' career really began to
　　take off.

10　Their first record, 'Love me do', was issued in October, 1962. Four months
　　later their second, 'Please, please me', went straight into the top ten and soon

reached the coveted number one spot, while their first L.P. became the fastest-selling L.P. of 1963. Although the group broke up, millionaires all, years ago, their records still sell all over the world. What is it that made the Beatles
15   special?

As a group they were competent and their voices were pleasant, but this would not have been enough. They were probably lucky in their influences: the rich Merseyside environment from which they sprang, combined with an admiration for black American rhythm-and-blues; and they were fortunate in
20   the rapport that they found with one another and with their audience, while the songwriting partnership of Lennon and McCartney produced a stream of brilliant hits.

Their themes were precisely those that occupied and concerned their young audience: love, sorrow, good luck, bad luck and the quaint characters that are
25   always to be found in any big city. In addition they created melodies that were rich and original enough to be played and sung by musicians of the calibre of Count Basie and Ella Fitzgerald.

The Beatles were special because they believed in their own talents. They copied no-one, and they were strong enough not to allow themselves to be
30   destroyed by the overnight achievement of success beyond the reach of the imagination. In this they probably owed much to their record producer George Martin and their manager Brian Epstein.

A   Questions

1   How did Lennon die?
2   What was Paul McCartney doing in Hamburg?
3   Can you explain the expression 'the top ten'? (line 11)
4   What sort of music did the Beatles enjoy listening to?
5   Can you explain the expression 'the rich Merseyside environment'? (line 18)
6   Why do you think the Beatles understood their fans so well?
7   Where do you think the Beatles got their inspiration from?
8   What can you say about the subject matter of the songs written by Lennon and McCartney?
9   How exactly did the Beatles make their money?
10   What does the writer mean when he writes of somebody being 'destroyed by the achievement of success'? (line 30) In what way could a person be 'destroyed by success'?

B   Vocabulary exercise

1   Did you collect *autographs* when you were young? Is there anyone whose autographed photograph you would like to have now?
2   How do young doctors who have passed their exams *gain experience* in your country?
3   'Love me do' was *issued* in 1962. What other things are issued?
4   The writer describes the Beatles as *competent* musicians. Competent means 'good but not fantastic'. Can you think of other people we might describe as competent?
5   The Beatles came from a working-class Merseyside *environment*. What are the different features that make up an environment?
6   Can you think of a *theme* that might provide a lively discussion between you and your friends?
7   The writer speaks of '*quaint* characters'. What other things might be described as quaint?
8   Lennon and McCartney *created* unforgettable tunes and topical lyrics. What does a novelist create?

Pop music

9 The Beatles were lucky because they found a way of using their *talents* in such a way that they were able to enjoy themselves and make a lot of money. But most people have talents, many of which are never used. What about you? Have you got any hidden talents?

10 What might *destroy* a farmer's crop of corn or olives or fruit or vegetables?

C   Vocabulary exercise

There are a great number of words and phrases in English that belong together. Fluent speakers and writers must learn to recognise and use them. In the account of the Beatles, the author tells us that John Lennon was *murdered* outside his apartment. There are many other words that could mean almost the same but are not appropriate in this context. Here are three examples of words that are similar in meaning to 'murdered':

1   destroyed
2   assassinated
3   demolished

Of course, you can guess. However, if you want to be accurate you should use a dictionary and work with other students. Your task is to find out (a) why these words are not appropriate, (b) when they would be appropriate.

Here are some word problems for you to solve. Decide which of the answers is inappropriate in this context. One of the clues is in the Reading passage. Two of the answers are always inappropriate. Circle the appropriate answers.

1 John Lennon might have autographed a
  a contract.
  b record sleeve.
  c book.
  d cheque.

2 The Beatles first record was
  a published ⎫
  b edited   ⎬ in October, 1962.
  c issued   ⎭
  d brought out

3 As musicians they are
  a competent.
  b efficient.
  c business-like.
  d able.

4 Their themes occupied and
  a worried   ⎫
  b concerned ⎬ their young audience.
  c involved ⎭
  d disturbed

5 They
  a discovered   ⎫
  b manufactured ⎬ melodies that were rich
  c composed   ⎭ and original.
  d created

6 The Beatles
  a imitated   ⎫
  b counterfeited ⎬ no-one.
  c copied   ⎭
  d forged

7 They were probably lucky in their
  a cultural backgrounds.
  b influences.
  c wealth and power.
  d important positions.

D   Discussion

Do you like Beatles music?

Can you remember the title of any Beatles songs not mentioned in the text?

Are there any current pop tunes that you like very much?

Some people turn on the radio and listen to pop music as soon as they wake up in the morning; others hate pop music; others just don't mind it. Which group do you belong to?

What do you think of the current fashion for 'background music' in shops, hotels and restaurants? Does it ever annoy you or do you like it?

E   Practice activity

Study this conversation:

Tom and Hilda were discussing Beatles songs.

HILDA   What's your favourite Beatles song?
TOM   'Till there was you'.
HILDA   I haven't heard that one.
TOM   Do you know 'A hard day's night'?
HILDA   Oh yes, I've often heard that on the radio. I heard it this morning, actually.
TOM   I think 'Till there was you' is in the same album.

UNIT 2 Pop music

Hilda uses the *present perfect* tense:

I haven't heard that one.
I've often heard that on the radio.

until she introduces the *point in time* 'this morning'. Then she uses the *simple past* tense.

Use these ideas connected with the Beatles to produce more sentences in the *present perfect* or the *simple past*.

Example: 'She loves me'
I've heard 'She loves me' many times on the radio.
Have you ever heard the song 'She loves me'?
I've never even heard of the song 'She loves me'.
They played 'She loves me' on the radio yesterday.

1   The film 'Magical Mystery Tour'.
2   A picture of the Beatles.
3   The 'Sergeant Pepper' album.
4   'Penny Lane'.
5   Liverpool.
6   Lennon and McCartney.
7   Yoko Ono (Lennon's wife).
8   The Cavern.

F   Practice activity

Peter wants to hear people talking with some different English accents.

We can say:
If *he goes* to Liverpool, *he'll be able to hear* people talking with a Liverpool accent.

Continue in the same way:

1   John wants to hear people talking Russian.
2   Linda wants to eat French food.
3   James wants to take photographs of wild elephants.
4   Monica wants to hear Hawaiian music.
5   David wants to see some Egyptian mummies.
6   Sarah wants to see some olive trees.
7   Arnold wants to see a Grand Prix motor race.
8   Steve wants to see some Buddhist temples.

G   Practice activity

Study this pattern:

They issued the record 'Love me do' in 1962.
The record 'Love me do' was issued in 1962.

Brian Epstein managed the Beatles.
The Beatles were managed by Brian Epstein.

Practise making passives:

1   The Beatles made the film 'Magical Mystery Tour'.
2   People all over the world still buy Beatles records.
3   Lennon and McCartney wrote a lot of the best Beatles songs.
4   Ella Fitzgerald sang several of their songs.
5   You can always find quaint characters in any big city.
6   Millions of people saw the Beatles on television.
7   Count Basie recorded 'Can't buy me love'.
8   Musicians still play rock music in Liverpool.

Dialogue 📼

Simon and Bob are brothers. At the moment they are sharing a room.
Before you listen to their conversation *study* the impression questions. While you listen to their conversation *think about* the impression questions. After you have listened *discuss* your impressions.

H   Impression questions

1   What is the difference in the brothers' musical taste?
2   Are Simon and Bob having an argument or a discussion?

3   Which of the brothers sounds sarcastic?
4   Which of the brothers uses the most intelligent arguments?
5   Should Bob have agreed to turn off the radio?

I   Focus questions

In the dialogue, there are several examples of sarcasm. Remember that Simon is talking to his younger brother and whenever he is extremely polite, he is usually being sarcastic. For example,

Pop music

Simon says, 'Do you think you could possibly turn off that radio?' He would normally say, 'How about turning off that radio?' or 'Turn off that radio, will you?'

Listen to the dialogue again and find more examples of sarcasm. Listen to the intonation rather than the words.

J   Focus questions

Listen to these examples of remarks and questions that look identical when they are written. Decide from the intonation whether the speakers are being polite or sarcastic. *Study the written questions and remarks first.* Do they seem to be polite?

1   Do you think you could possibly move your car?
2   Would you mind making your own bed?
3   How kind of you to look after my cat!
4   Could you give me a few minutes of your valuable time?
5   You know everything, don't you?

K   Focus questions

Now that you have studied the questions, look at further information and listen. Then write the words 'polite' or 'sarcastic'.

1   A traffic warden is speaking.
2   Simon is talking to Bob.
3   Simon's mother is talking to her elderly neighbour.
4   Simon's father is talking to his employer.
5   Simon's mother is talking to his father.

L   Discussion

Musical tastes vary. Simon likes classical music and Bob likes pop. What sort of music do you like?

If you are keen on pop, make a short list of bands or groups that you admire.

If you are keen on classical music, make a short list of the composers whose works you enjoy.

What do you think about Simon's remark: 'I'm not interested in what it's all about'?

Bob says: 'Pop music is the classical music of today.' Is there any truth in this?

Listening activity 📼

M   Comprehension

Here are eight statements referring to the interview. Decide whether they are true or false:

1   Andy Shaw works for a small record company.
2   Andy says you can make a lot of money out of pop music.
3   Musicians often send demo tapes to record companies.
4   When there is a big hit, a lot of other musicians try and copy the sound.
5   Andy knows exactly what makes a big hit.
6   It is possible to buy an L.P. with a big hit and other tunes on it.
7   It isn't easy to forecast which records are going to be very popular.
8   A lot of money is spent on promoting new artists.

N   Gap dictation

Here is part of the C.B.C. radio conversation with important words missing.

Listen to the conversation again and write the missing words.

ANDY   But the number one hit is the one with instant appeal, the theme that (1)_____.
ROBIN   And luck (2)_____, doesn't it?
ANDY   Of course. The Beatles (3)_____ by one of the biggest record companies in the business and they (4)_____ make millions. It's an extraordinarily difficult task picking the numbers which are (5)_____ the charts.
ROBIN   And a great deal of money (6)_____ on promotion, isn't it?

O   Writing activity

Listen to the interview again and make notes. Answer these questions and then summarise the points that Andy Shaw makes.

1   Can you still make a lot of money out of pop music?
2   What do musicians normally send to record companies these days?
3   Is it easy to tell if a tune is going to be a big hit?
4   What do record companies have to do to promote new records?
5   How are record companies sometimes surprised?

P   Writing activity

Andy Shaw obviously takes pop music very seriously.

Very often it is young people who like the latest pop music, while older people don't. Why do you think this happens?

Think about the part that pop music plays in people's lives. Do you remember what Bob said when he was talking to Simon? He said 'Pop music is the classical music of today'. Write a paragraph of 120–150 words agreeing or disagreeing with Bob's statement.

Summary

In this unit we compare the use of the *present perfect* tense:

I've heard that song.

with the *simple past* tense:
I heard that song on the radio last night.

Explain why the *present perfect* is used in the first example, while the *simple past* is used in the second.

We also practise using the *first conditional* pattern:

If you go to Edinburgh, *you will hear* people speaking with a Scottish accent. Why do we begin some sentences with 'If' and others with 'When'?

We practise, too, making simple *passive* sentences:

Examples:
John Lennon was murdered.
A lot of the best Beatles songs were written by Lennon and McCartney.

What is the most important fact in each of these two sentences?

UNIT 3　Holidays

Reading activity

PETER AND ELIZABETH

1　Peter and Elizabeth hadn't been married for long. They had both been
working very hard, so Peter thought it would be a good idea to give Elizabeth
a little surprise.

He noticed an advertisement for cheap sunshine holidays in Spain. Without
5　telling Elizabeth what he was planning to do, he booked seats on a flight
leaving at midnight on the next Thursday evening. Then he went home,
looking very cheerful.
'Darling,' he said, 'you'd better tell your boss you want a couple of extra days'
holiday.'
10　'Oh,' she said, 'are we going away?'
Proudly he laid the air tickets on the table.
'Spain,' she said, 'isn't that going to be terribly expensive?'
'It's all taken care of,' he said.

As soon as they got home from work on Thursday, they packed their suitcases,
15　tidied up the flat, had a meal, and set out for Gatwick Airport. They heard on
the radio that some flights had been delayed.

It was very cold. Snow was falling and the visibility was bad. Peter and
Elizabeth sat in the lounge at Gatwick all night waiting for news. Then they
were given breakfast and told to climb aboard a coach.
20　'We are going to Luton Airport,' they were told. 'Weather conditions are
better there.'

It took nearly three hours to reach Luton, but, by the time they got there, all
flights had been cancelled, so the company sent them to a hotel. They spent

23

25 Saturday at Luton Airport, hoping that the weather would change, but it didn't. Then came reports that conditions were improving in the north of England.

About six o'clock they were bundled into coaches and set off for Manchester. They arrived there some time after midnight. By now everyone was getting cross and miserable. Around tea-time on Sunday the visibility began to
30 improve, then suddenly more snow began to fall.

'Let's go home,' whispered Elizabeth. They collected their luggage, left the airport and caught a train back to London. They arrived home just before midnight.

Elizabeth lay in bed, looking up at the ceiling.
35 'My goodness,' she said sleepily, 'it's nice to be home.'

A   Questions

1 Ask how long Peter and Elizabeth had been married.
2 Answer the question.
3 Why was Peter looking happy when he got home?
4 What had he done?
5 What did he suggest that Elizabeth should tell her employer?
6 Did Peter go to work on Thursday?
7 Did Peter and Elizabeth hear anything interesting on the radio?
8 What did they learn when they arrived at Gatwick Airport?
9 Where did they spend Thursday night?
10 Ask how long it took them to get to Luton.
11 How did they travel to Manchester?
12 Was it dark when they got to Manchester?
13 How was everybody feeling?
14 Who suggested that they should go home?
15 How do you think Elizabeth felt when they got back home?

B   Vocabulary exercise

1 Where are you *planning* to go for your next holiday? What other plans might you make?
2 Peter *booked* seats on a flight to Spain. What other things could you book?
3 Is there any special time during the week when you look or feel especially *cheerful?*
4 Think of some things that might be described as '*terribly expensive*'.

5 Peter says: '*It's all taken care of*', meaning 'I have made all the necessary arrangements'. Think of some more situations where this expression might be useful.
6 Before Peter and Elizabeth left home, they *tidied up* their flat. What other things could you tidy up?
7 All flights were *cancelled* because of the snow. Think of some other things that might be cancelled and the reasons for the cancellation.
8 The passengers were *cross and miserable* because they had been waiting for aeroplanes and sitting for hours in a coach. What sort of things make you cross and miserable? Have you felt like this recently? Why?

C   Vocabulary exercise

First find the word in the Reading passage that will complete the example sentence. Then choose *two* words from the following lists that you think are appropriate in this context.

1 Example sentence: He _____ an advertisement for holidays.
   a published
   b observed
   c called attention to
   d saw

2 Example sentence: 'It's all _____,' he said.
   a arranged
   b provided
   c paid for
   d looked after

Holidays

3 Example sentence: Peter and Elizabeth were
_____ to climb aboard a coach.
  a ordered
  b informed
  c instructed
  d asked

4 Example sentence: Some flights had been
_____.
  a put back
  b put away
  c put off
  d put down

5 Example sentence: Then came _____ that
conditions were improving.
  a documents
  b information
  c news
  d correspondence

6 Example sentence: They spent Saturday at
Luton Airport hoping that the _____ would
change.
  a climate
  b conditions
  c atmosphere
  d situation

D Discussion

Peter and Elizabeth are planning a holiday with
two friends, but they can't decide which sort of
holiday to choose. Here are the different kinds of
holiday they have been considering:

  a A motoring holiday, travelling from place to
    place, never knowing where you're going to
    spend the next night.
  b A camping holiday, where you stay at an
    organised camping site.
  c A holiday at the seaside, where you stay in a
    nice hotel, swim every day and meet new
    friends.
  d A holiday in a big city like Paris, where you
    spend your time visiting galleries and
    museums and eating in beautiful restaurants.

*Which holiday would you choose? Put them in order of
preference and say why.*

E Practice activity

Elizabeth whispered 'Let's go home.' (line 31)
Elizabeth suggested (that) they should go home.

What other suggestions were made?

1 Elizabeth said: 'Let's have a cup of coffee.'
2 Peter said: 'Let's go and look at the bookstall.'
3 Elizabeth said: 'Let's buy something to read.'
4 Peter said: 'Let's go and get some fresh air.'
5 Elizabeth said: 'Let's go and look at the flight
    departures board.'
6 Peter said: 'Let's find out when the next train
    leaves for London.'

F Practice activity

Peter said to Elizabeth: 'It's all taken care of.'
(line 13)
Peter told Elizabeth (that) it was all taken care of.

What else did Peter and Elizabeth tell people?

1 Elizabeth said to her friends in the office:
    'We're going to Spain for a holiday.'
2 Peter said to his boss: 'Package holidays like
    the one we are going on aren't expensive.'
3 Elizabeth said to Peter: 'I'm afraid the weather
    forecast isn't very good.'
4 Peter said to Elizabeth: 'They can clear the
    snow off the runway very quickly.'
5 Peter said to Elizabeth: 'They have radar at all
    major airports now.'
6 An announcement was made over the loud-
    speaker system, but Elizabeth didn't hear it.
    Peter said: 'All flights are cancelled.'

G Practice activity

Libby and Daphne worked in the same office as
Elizabeth. After Elizabeth told them what Peter
had done, Libby said to Daphne: 'How would you
feel if your husband bought tickets for a holiday in
Spain, without asking you first?'
'I'd be furious,' replied Daphne.

Ask and answer some more questions:
1 How would you feel if a stranger came up to
    you in the street and asked for your autograph?
2 How would you feel if your boss told you he
    was going to raise your salary?
3 How would you feel if your dentist said he
    must take out three of your front teeth?
4 How would you feel if someone borrowed and
    then lost one of your favourite records?
5 How would you feel if a film producer offered
    you a part in a film?
6 How would you feel if someone pointed a gun
    at you and demanded your money?

7 How would you feel if you got a job in the toy department of a big store and they made you dress up in a rabbit costume?

8 How would you feel if you won a free holiday in India in a travel competition?

H Practice activity

John wants a copy of the L.P. 'A hard day's night', but finds that it has been deleted from the catalogue. The assistant in the record shop says: 'If I were you, I'd try at a shop that sells second-hand records.'

Practise giving advice using: 'If I were you . . . '

1 John's friend Malcolm has been having very bad headaches. Up till now he has just taken aspirins. John says: _____.

2 Sonia has a boyfriend who has been behaving very badly, not turning up for dates and going out with other girls. Sonia's friend Esther says: _____.

3 Your friend Roger has had a car for six years. It wasn't new when he bought it and now it is costing him a lot in repair bills. You say: _____.

4 Your friend Simone is a very good secretary, but she dislikes her boss intensely. You say: _____.

5 Paul bought a pair of binoculars. He wasn't very happy with them and he showed them to Tom. Tom thinks they are faulty. He says: _____.

6 Maria is Brazilian. She is in London and wants to visit France. However, she doesn't know if she needs a visa. You say: _____.

Dialogue 🔊

Peter and Stephanie have been working for the same company for several years. They are standing in a queue at the company cafeteria. Before you listen to them, study the impression questions.

I Impression questions

1 Do you think Peter and Stephanie are friends or acquaintances?

2 Why is Peter asking so many questions?

3 How does Stephanie avoid answering some of Peter's questions?

4 Do you think Stephanie is interested in Peter's plans?

5 Do you think Stephanie is married?

6 What about Peter? Is he married?

7 Have Stephanie and Peter got many common interests?

Now listen to the conversation. Think about the Impression questions and listen again to the conversation before you discuss your impressions.

J   Focus questions

Study these examples from the conversation.

PETER   That'll cost a bit, won't it?
STEPHANIE   Not really. We've got friends who live
            there.
PETER   That is good organisation.
STEPHANIE   Yes it is, isn't it?

Practise asking and answering the questions. Notice whether your voice rises or falls at the end of the questions. Decide whether both questions are asking for information.

K   Now look at more examples of conversations and decide whether the voices should rise or fall at the end of the question.

1   PETER   We haven't met for a long time,
                    have we?
        STEPHANIE   Not really.

2   PETER   You still work in the Accounts
                    Department, don't you?
        STEPHANIE   Yes, I've been there for two years
                    now.

3   PETER   Your boss has just retired, hasn't
                    he?
        STEPHANIE   You know he has.

4   PETER   You're not very friendly, are you?
        STEPHANIE   What do you expect?

5   PETER   I'll see you here tomorrow, won't
                    I?
        STEPHANIE   No, I'm afraid not. I'm going to
                    bring a few sandwiches from now
                    on.

Now practise asking and answering the questions yourselves.

L   Discussion

Imagine you have friends who live in *one* of the following places. You have the opportunity of going to spend your summer holiday with them.

Cannes (south of France)
Rome (Italy)
Edinburgh (Scotland)
Benidorm (Spain)
St Moritz (Switzerland)

In which place would you most like to have friends you could go and stay with? Put them in order of preference and say why.

Listening activity 🔲

M   Comprehension

Here are eight statements referring to the interview. Decide whether they are true or false:

1   Some people think holidays in Britain are too dear.
2   Travellers arriving at Victoria Station all have large packs on their backs.
3   It is impossible to have a pleasant holiday in Britain without spending a lot of money.
4   Students can earn a lot of money working as receptionists at a hostel.
5   Three German boys spent the night in the grounds of Buckingham Palace.
6   Hostels are less expensive than hotels.
7   The N.U.S. provides an information service for students.
8   These days students don't hitch lifts when they are alone.

N   Gap dictation

Here is part of the interview, with certain words missing. Listen to this part of the interview and write the missing words.

RUPERT STONE:
I don't think we really need to (1)_____. We keep lists of hostels providing (2)_____, naturally, and we have (3)_____ regarding cheap travel and (4)_____. But it's really (5)_____, isn't it? If you are (6)_____ and you (7)_____ restaurant, your (8)_____ is going to cost you £3 or £4. But you can buy (9)_____ and (10)_____ for £1. If you stay at a hotel, you can pay the earth. If you sleep in a hostel, the price will be (11)_____, and if you're really (12)_____, then you just have to find a quiet corner and (13)_____ your sleeping bag.

O Writing activity

Listen to the interview again. What points does
Rupert Stone make?

P Writing activity

It seems sensible that British students should be
prepared to help students from abroad when they
come to visit Britain.

What useful information would you give to
English-speaking students about how to exist in
your country without spending too much money?

Summary

In this unit we begin our revision of *reported speech*.

Example:
'The weather in Jersey is fantastic.'
He said the weather in Jersey was fantastic.
or He told me (that) the weather in Jersey was
fantastic.

What happens to verbs in the present when the
reporting verb is in the past?

We also practise turning suggestions into *reported
speech*.

Example:
Peter: 'Let's go to the pictures'.
Peter suggested (that) we should go to the pictures.

We practise using the *second conditional*, answering
questions beginning:

'How would you feel if . . . ?'

Example:
How would you feel if you got the sack tomorrow?
I wouldn't mind much *or* I'd be very worried.

UNIT 4   School

Dulwich College

Reading activity

THE PRIVATE SYSTEM OF EDUCATION IN BRITAIN

1   Graham Cunliffe was head of a big comprehensive school for six years. He recently resigned from this post and has just been appointed headmaster of a much smaller independent school. When asked why he had switched to the private sector, he gave this reply:

5   'Over the past thirty years, millions of pounds have been spent on improving the free State education system in Britain. Many magnificent new schools have been built and enormous care has been taken to ensure that children are offered every opportunity to develop whatever talents they possess and to see that they receive the maximum benefit from the time they spend at school.

10   There is no doubt that educational opportunities are incomparably greater than they used to be. In spite of this, some 5 per cent of the population reject the State system and stubbornly persist in paying considerable sums in school fees for the privilege of sending their children to private schools. Why?

    The answer is probably very simple. If you want your son or daughter to be
15   reasonably certain of obtaining a top job or a comfortable position in one of the professions, the private system of education is still the surest path to the achievement of that aim.

    Does this mean that you will find more brilliant teachers in the private sector?

20 Not necessarily. However, you will almost certainly find a higher ratio of teachers to pupils and you will discover a single-minded determination on the part of the staff to see that members of the school obtain the 'O' and 'A' level examination results that are the necessary passport to university or one of the professions.

25 Virtually all the pupils in private schools go on to take 'O' and 'A' level examinations. They stay at school till they are 17 or 18 years old. In most State schools, a large proportion of the children leave at the age of 16. Thus the quest for success in public examinations is not followed with the same zeal as it is in the private sector; and the fact that many children are geared to leaving school at the earliest possible opportunity may well prove a disruptive 30 influence.

In Britain today the opportunity is there for any child with sufficient talent to enter a university and embark upon a successful career in any profession that he or she may choose. However, it is an undeniable fact that the private sector still offers the easiest route to the top.'

A Questions

1 Do most people in Britain pay school fees?
2 Is education in England better or worse than it used to be?
3 Why do some parents still send their children to private schools?
4 Where does the writer think you will find the cleverest teachers?
5 What is the main aim of teachers in the private sector?
6 Apart from the teaching, what advantage is there in sending your children to a private school?
7 Does the writer believe there is 'equal opportunity' in Britain today?

B Vocabulary exercise

1 A new school can be *magnificent*. What else might we describe as magnificent?
2 A good school tries to see that the children *develop* their talents. What other things might a person develop?
3 Five per cent of parents *reject* the state system. Why are some chocolates rejected in a chocolate factory? What do you think happens to these rejects?
4 Parents pay *fees* to a private school. Who else might a person pay a fee or fees to?
5 Why is it a good thing if a school has a high *ratio* of teachers to pupils?

6 How might a pupil in a class prove to be a *disruptive influence*?
7 Can you explain 'many children are *geared to leaving school* at the earliest possible opportunity'? (line 28)
8 Read the last sentence in the text. Can you think of any more '*undeniable facts*'?

C Vocabulary exercise

Look at the possible answers. Then look for the key word in the Reading passage. When you have found the key word, find the only word in the exercise that cannot be used in this context.

1 Enormous care has been taken to ensure that children are offered every _____ to develop whatever talent they possess. (line 7)
   a chance
   b luck
   c possibility
   d opportunity

2 Some 5 per cent of the population reject the State system and _____ paying considerable sums in school fees. (line 11)
   a go on
   b insist on
   c depend on
   d persist in

3 The answer is probably very _____. (line 14)

   a simple
   b stupid
   c easy
   d plain

4 If you want your son or daughter to be reasonably _____ of obtaining a top job. (line 14)

   a certain
   b guaranteed
   c assured
   d sure

5 _____ point is that virtually all the pupils in private schools go on to take 'O' and 'A' level exams. (line 24)

   a A farther
   b A further
   c An additional
   d Another

Now use your dictionaries to discover how words develop and change. Also decide whether there are differences in pronunciation. Here is an example:

Noun	Verb	Adjective
educator	*educate*	educational
1 comfort		
2	succeed	
3		reasonable
4 interest		
5		admirable

D Discussion

Do you have state schools and private schools in your country?

Do a lot of children go to private schools? What benefits do they get?

What are the examinations that boys and girls have to take in your country? How old are they when they take them?

Do you think there is 'equal opportunity' in your country? Give reasons for your answer.

E Practice activity

We can say:
The State has spent millions of pounds on education.

However, sometimes we can express the same idea more clearly by using the passive:

Millions of pounds have been spent (by the State) on education.

Make more passives:
1 The school has recently built a fine new gymnasium.
2 We have just raised our fees for the first time in five years.
3 A parent has just presented a *Complete Works of Charles Dickens* to the school.
4 We have taken great care to design a school in which it will be a pleasure to study.
5 We have asked all our parents to encourage their children to stay at school as long as possible.
6 What a nuisance! Someone has broken one of the windows in the Headmaster's study.

F Practice activity

We can say:
You will find brilliant teachers in the State schools and in the private schools too.

However, sometimes we can express the idea more forcefully by using the passive:

Brilliant teachers will be found in the State schools and in the private schools too.

Continue in the same way:
1 The photographer will take the school photograph on Monday afternoon.
2 We shall play the football match against Forest Hill School next Wednesday afternoon.
3 In future, we shall teach French to first-year pupils.
4 Starting next week, we shall open the canteen half an hour earlier in the morning.
5 During the coming term, we shall show a film in the main hall every Friday evening at 7.30.
6 I shall certainly tell the Headmaster about your behaviour.

G Practice activity

Most pupils in private schools *go on* to take 'O' level and 'A' level exams. (line 24)

The verb 'go' is frequently used with prepositions

and adverbs.
For example:

We've received the goods, so you can *go ahead* and pay the account.
You promised. You can't *go back on* our agreement now.
Let's *go over* the plans again.
Tom and Jenny have been *going out together* for some months.
I don't want to *go into* the matter now.
He keeps *going on about* how badly he's paid.
She *went without* food or water for nearly three days.
I'd like to *go through* the accounts with you tomorrow morning.
The dog *went for* the cat, but the cat shot up the nearest tree.

Replace the words in italics by suitable expressions with 'go' from the list above. Use each expression once only:

1   Dr Jordan has examined the X-rays and he's ready to *proceed* with the operation.
2   I didn't know Dick had been *complaining* about having too much work to do.
3   I'd like to *check* the security arrangements you've made for the President's visit next week.
4   I don't want to *examine* the question of costs till tomorrow.
5   How long have Tim and Daphne been *keeping company*?
6   I don't want you to *deny yourself* your usual cup of coffee, just because I don't like it.

Dialogue 🔘

Irmgaard is visiting England for the fourth time. She and her friend, Phillipa, first met on a school exchange visit. Obviously, both girls are older than they were when they first met and situations and problems have changed.
Before you listen to their conversation, study the Impression questions. After you have listened, discuss the Impression questions. Remember that you may not agree with other people's impressions.

H   Impression questions

1   Why was Irmgaard sitting in the dark?
2   Did Phillipa really know why Irmgaard had come to England?
3   What were the problems Irmgaard was facing?
4   Do you think Phillipa helped Irmgaard to solve her problems?
5   When do you think Irmgaard should get in touch with her parents?

I   Focus questions

Irmgaard didn't want to discuss her problems when Phillipa came in. She said: 'I'm all right.' She was avoiding the problem.
Phillipa said: 'But what are you trying to do?' She was asking for an answer.

Practise saying these remarks with attention to the intonation.

Now study these questions. Decide whether they need answers.
You should listen to the dialogue after you have made your decision.

1   You can't even see them, can you?
2   You're not looking very happy, are you?
3   What's the matter?
4   Why don't you make some coffee?
5   That's better, isn't it?
6   What's the problem exactly?
7   Do you really want to study in England?
8   We'll need a map, won't we?

Now give the answers you think are suitable.

J   Discussion

Here are the three advertisements that Irmgaard and Phillipa are looking at:

Imagine *you* were helping Irmgaard to choose a school. Look carefully at the three advertisements.

Divide into groups and make a list of the advantages and disadvantages of each school.

Choose a spokesman to report your conclusions to the rest of the class.

The Oak School of English

A small, friendly school situated in a fine old house in beautiful countryside, five miles from St Albans.

Capacity: 70 students (not more than 10 of any one nationality).

30 hours tuition weekly. Classes not bigger than 10.

Accommodation in the school (double rooms).

4-week course: Price £420.

The Beech School of English

A medium-sized school situated in North London, twenty minutes from the centre by Underground.

Capacity: 140 students.

24 hours tuition weekly. Classes up to 14.

Accommodation in student hostel.

Full programme of visits to theatre, ballet, places of interest arranged by the school.

4-week course: Price £320.

The Pines School of English

A large, modern purpose-built school, situated near the sea front at Eastbourne, a pleasant seaside resort.

Capacity: 300 students.

20 hours tuition weekly. Usual class size 15.

Accommodation with carefully-selected English families.

Language laboratory, tennis, sailing, swimming.

4-week course: Price £310.

Listening activity 🎧

K Comprehension

1 Who was the caller?
2 What has Margaret just received?
3 Is the programme of classes the same as it was last year?
4 Which class is Margaret going to attend on a Monday evening?
5 What is Margaret going to do on a Tuesday evening?
6 When does the 'Keep-fit' class take place?
7 Which class is Neil going to attend on a Monday evening?
8 Which class are Margaret and Neil going to go to together?

L Gap dictation

Listen to a part of Margaret's conversation with Neil. First read the Gap dictation exercise and try to remember what was said. Then listen for the missing words. You will have enough time to write the answers, but you can ask your teacher to repeat the conversation if you miss something.

MARGARET Look, I've just got the prospectus for (1)_____ evening classes. You said (2)_____ to come again, so (3)_____ if we (4)_____ go to one or two classes together.

NEIL Oh, that's a good idea. Is the programme (5)_____ last year?

MARGARET More or less. (6)_____ new classes.

M Writing activity

Here is Neil Shaw's enrolment form. His address is 21 Market Street, Harrow, Middlesex.

You fill in the form for him.

Surname		First names	
Address			
Date			
I wish to attend the following classes:			
Day	Time	Class	
1			
2			
3			
4			
5			
Signed:			
Note: 1 class weekly: £15 Each additional class: £5	Fee paid _____ Signed _____ (Secretary)		

N   Writing activity

The word 'schooldays' suggests different things to different people. The word might bring back a memory of an especially happy class, or a particular teacher, or lessons that you enjoyed or found very boring. What does the word suggest to you?

Discuss your schooldays with other students.

Write two paragraphs about your schooldays. In the first say what you liked. In the second say what you didn't like. You will need about 300 words.

Summary

In this unit we continue our revision of the *passive* voice, using the *present perfect* tense.

Example:
We have arranged a meeting of the committee.
A meeting of the committee has been arranged.

We also practise turning *simple future* tense into the *passive*.

Example:
We shall announce our decision in due course.
Our decision will be announced in due course.

Note also these useful phrasal verbs with 'go':

to go ahead, to go back on, to go over, to go out (together), to go into, to go on (about something), to go without, to go through, to go for.

Give an example of something we might wish to *go over* and something we might have to *go without* if we were short of money.

UNIT 5   Ancestors

Edinburgh Castle

Reading activity

FAMILY HISTORY

1   My father was English, my mother Scottish, and I visited Scotland recently
    with the intention of discovering what I could about my Scottish ancestors.
    My grandmother's name was Renton. Her husband, my grandfather, spent
    most of his working life in India. After he died she came back to Scotland and
5   settled down with her sisters in an old house beside a golf course, in a village
    called Gullane. As a small boy I was taken to visit her there.

    I knew that my great-grandfather, my grandmother's father, had written a
    book about his experiences as a young minister in Canada, so I went to the
    National Library in Edinburgh to find out if they had a copy. However, the
10 visit was a disappointment. There were a number of Rentons in the catalogue.
    But I could find no reference to my great-grandfather's book.

    I also knew that after my great-grandfather had returned to Scotland from
    Canada, he had spent twenty years or more as Minister of the Presbyterian
    Church at North Berwick and my mother had told me that he had six
15 daughters, five of whom had never married.

    On a beautiful sunny Saturday morning I drove from Edinburgh to North
    Berwick. I found somewhere to park and asked the way to the church. My
    mother had told me of the minister's house and the minister's meadow, a small
    sloping field, where my grandfather kept a few cows, and where my grand-
20 mother and her five sisters had played as little girls. But this was seventy years
    ago.

    The street was narrow and busy with Saturday afternoon shoppers. I strolled
    along and suddenly there it was in front of me. St Andrew's Church. The
    main doors were locked, so I made my way to the back, found a small door that

25 was open, let myself in and looked round the church. The sunshine flooded
through the stained-glass windows and shone upon the brass memorial
plaques on the walls. But I looked in vain for the name Renton. Then it struck
me that Renton was my grandmother's *married* name. Before that her name
was . . . was . . . Sprott. Of course. No wonder I hadn't been able to find my
30 great-grandfather's book in the library. I looked again and soon I found a
stained-glass window and a plaque 'In memory of the Rev. George Washing-
ton Sprott, Minister of this kirk . . . '

Behind the church, at the top of a small hill, the minister's house still stood
and between the house and the church lay the small sloping meadow where
35 my grandmother used to play among the cows. There were no cows there now,
but in one corner, standing in the shade of a tree, was a hot, grey, bored-
looking donkey.

The following Monday I returned to the National Library in Edinburgh and
there I found my great-grandfather's book, *Reflections on the Life of a Young*
40 *Minister in Canada*, by the Rev. G. W. Sprott. It was dedicated to 'My
children and their children's children'.

A Questions

1 Why did the writer go to Scotland?
2 How did he travel about Scotland?
3 Why couldn't he find his great-grandfather's
book when he went to the National Library?
4 What did the writer hope to find in North
Berwick?
5 What did he find in North Berwick?

B Vocabulary exercise

1 The writer's grandmother *settled down* in Scotland. Can you think of any situations in which
you might ask a friend if he or she has settled
down?
2 We don't *drive* a motor-bike, an aeroplane or a
yacht. What word do we use with each of these
forms of transport?
3 What sort of things do people *reminisce* over?
4 The *main* doors were locked. Can you think
about some other things about which we might
use the word 'main'?
5 A *meadow* is a sort of field. What sort?
6 Why would it be difficult to play football on a
sloping field?
7 The windows were made of *stained* glass. What
sort of things might stain a white tablecloth?
8 What would you expect to find on a *memorial
plaque* in a church?
9 What sort of things are made of *brass*?

10 *Reflections on the Life of a Young Minister.* Here
the reflections were thoughts. Where might
you expect to see your reflection?

C Vocabulary exercise

This exercise gives sentences from the Reading
passage with the key word in *italics*. Your task is to
find two of the four choices that could replace this
word or phrase. Remember that two of the four will
be inappropriate in this context.

1 I visited Scotland recently with the intention of
discovering what I could. (line 1)
a inventing
b learning
c realising
d finding out

2 She came back to Scotland and *settled down*
with her sisters. (line 4)
a rested
b made her home
c became familiar
d moved in

3 There were a number of Rentons in the *catalogue*. (line 10)
a brochure
b list
c file
d agenda

4   I asked where I might *find* the church. (line 17)
     a   discover
     b   come across
     c   look for
     d   encounter

5   Then it *struck* me that Renton was my grand-mother's married name. (line 27)
     a   attacked
     b   hit
     c   occurred to
     d   impressed

6   The *main* doors were locked. (line 23)
     a   strong
     b   principal
     c   principle
     d   chief

D   Discussion

What sort of things would you like to know about your ancestors?
Sit down with a friend and make a list.

You can pay quite a lot of money to get a professional firm to enquire into your family history. How do you think these firms go about obtaining information? What questions would they ask? Who might they ask? Where do you think they might go for information?

E   Practice activity

Read this report from the store detective to the manager of a supermarket:
Tuesday, 7th November.

At 9.30 a.m. this morning Mrs Ada Piddock, aged 42, of 17 Datchet Road, reported that her purse had been stolen in the store. She felt sure that the purse had been taken by two young men. Mrs Piddock remembered that she checked in her purse when she reached the cheese counter to see if she had remembered to bring a discount ticket which she had cut out of the newspaper. She then placed her purse on top of her shopping in the wire basket. At the time the two young men were standing nearby and she also noticed a lady with an eighteen-month old baby in a pram beside her. As soon as Mrs Piddock reached the checkout and discovered that her purse was missing, I was called and was given a description of the two young men. I looked for the lady with the baby, but she had already left the supermarket. I circulated a description of the suspects to all staff and warned them to be on the alert. After Mrs Piddock had left the store, her purse was found on the floor near the cheese counter. Her money was still inside the purse. I therefore informed the staff that the young men were no longer under suspicion.

Now follow these instructions

  1   Ask what time Mrs Piddock reported that her purse had been stolen.
  2   Ask why she noticed the two young men.
  3   Why did she think the young men had stolen her purse?
  4   Ask why she checked in her purse.
  5   Answer the question.
  6   How did she obtain the discount ticket?
  7   Ask where she put her purse.
  8   Ask when Mrs Piddock found that her purse was missing.
  9   Answer the question.
10   Why do you think the store detective looked for the lady with the baby?
11   What do you think had happened to Mrs Piddock's purse?
12   Why did the store detective inform the staff that the two young men were no longer under suspicion?

F   Practice activity

Example:
The Manager wanted to know if anyone had found the missing purse.
He said: 'Has the missing purse been found?'

You continue.

1   Then he wanted to know if anyone had informed the police.
     He said: 'Have the . . .'

2   They told him that someone had telephoned the police. The Manager wanted to know if they'd given a description of the two young men to the police.
     He said 'Has a . . .'

3   Then it occurred to the Manager that the purse might still be somewhere in the store. He wanted to know if they'd searched the store thoroughly.
     He asked the question: 'Has the . . .'

4 About half an hour later a policeman arrived. He wanted to know if anyone had seen the two young men in the store before.
He said: 'Have the . . .'

5 Then the policeman asked the Manager if any other customers had lost their purses recently.
He said: 'Have . . . stolen?'

6 Eventually Moira Pratt, a junior assistant, found the purse underneath the cheese counter. She handed it to the Manager. Shortly afterwards, the policeman asked if anybody had told the lady who lost the purse.
He said: 'Has the . . .'

7 So the Manager explained that Miss Pratt had only just found the purse.
He said: 'The purse . . .'

8 Then he telephoned Mrs Piddock:
He said: 'I've got some good news for you.
Your . . .'

G Practice activity

Note this phrase from the Reading activity: 'and *looked round* the church'. (line 25)

The verb 'look' is frequently used with prepositions and adverbs.

For example:

Could you possibly *look after* my daughter for an hour or so while I do some shopping?

Oh, I like your shoes. I've been *looking for* a really comfortable pair for ages.

Look out, there's a car coming.

Are you coming to see the play?
Yes, I'm *looking forward to* it very much.

Have you heard anything about your stolen car?
Not yet. But the police are *looking into* this matter.

I'd like you to *look through* these photographs and see if you can recognise any of the men.

I just want to *look up* the meaning of this word.

I hope you'll *look in* any time you're passing.

A party of visitors are coming to *look round* the factory tomorrow afternoon

Replace the words in italics by suitable expressions with 'look'. Use each expression once only:

1 Good afternoon. I'm *trying to find* someone called Baker.
2 The people next door are very kind. They *took care of* our cat while we were away on holiday.
3 '*Be careful*,' said Don, 'there seems to be something lying in the road.'
4 We visited the castle and *inspected* the sixteenth-century kitchen.
5 Oh, I forgot to tell you, John *called* this morning.
6 Could you possibly *examine* these old magazines this weekend and see if there are any you want to keep? I'm going to throw the others away.

Dialogue 📼

Brian and Valerie have been friends for years, although they haven't met for some time. Brian has developed a new interest and he is telling Valerie all about it. Study the Impression questions. When you listen to their conversation, you will know how to answer.

H Impression questions

1 Where do you think Brian and Valerie are at the moment?
2 What would you say Brian's new interest is?
3 Does Valerie share his interest?
4 How much attention is Brian paying to Valerie?
5 Do you think Valerie understands everything Brian is saying?
6 Is Valerie polite to Brian?
7 Do you think Valerie is stupid?
8 What about Brian? Is he boring?

Now listen to the conversation again. Answer the questions and give reasons for your impressions.

I Focus questions

Study these examples from the dialogue. Look at the words in *italics* and decide which other words you could substitute from this list:
hope know imagine believe think predict assume

PETER   It was there, stuck in his sacrum.
VALERIE I *suppose* that's what killed him.

PETER   Even walking must have been difficult. I wonder how he managed.
VALERIE I *expect* the other members of his tribe looked after him.

PETER   They can't have been quite so uncivilised as we imagine, can they?
VALERIE I *suppose* not.

Check your answers with your teacher before you try to do the next part.

J Focus questions

Now practise using these expressions, and work with a neighbour, Here are two examples:

Situation   You think Stone-Age people were very inventive. Your neighbour agrees.
YOU   'Stone-Age people must bave been very inventive.'
NEIGHBOUR   'I _____ so.'

Situation   You think Stone-Age women didn't have an easy life.
YOU   'Stone-Age women couldn't have had an easy life.'
NEIGHBOUR   'I _____ not.'

Now you do it:

1 *Situation*   You think Stone-Age children didn't have much security.
   YOU
   NEIGHBOUR

2 *Situation*   You think Stone-Age families had a very limited diet.
   YOU
   NEIGHBOUR

3 *Situation*   You think prehistoric people didn't live to be very old.
   YOU
   NEIGHBOUR

4 *Situation*   You think prehistoric people were much smaller than people today.
   YOU
   NEIGHBOUR

5 *Situation*   You think prehistoric families didn't have the same problems that families have today.
   YOU
   NEIGHBOUR

K Discussion

Think of the life of a small tribe of Stone-Age men, women and children. They hunted for food; they had no agriculture, no domestic animals. They probably had to change their camp fairly frequently.

What do you think their lives were like? What were their daily priorities? When they chose a new camp, what do you think they were looking for?

What do you think about Brian's remark: 'They can't have been quite so uncivilised as we imagine, can they?'

At some point in the development of each civilisation, language must have started. The first words probably referred to objects. What 'objects' do you think the first ten words might have referred to?

Listening activity 🔘

L   Comprehension

Here are six statements referring to the interview.
Decide whether they are true or false:

1   Anyone is allowed to examine old birth certificates.
2   It is always easy to find out when people got married.
3   More information is usually available about rich families than poor families.
4   Firms like the one Laura works for sometimes discover facts that might embarrass their clients.
5   Most families have ancestors who were pirates or highwaymen.
6   People usually get upset if you tell them that one of their relations was a criminal.

M   Gap dictation

First look at the Gap dictation and think of the words and phrases you have just heard. You will need to listen to groups of words and *think* of them as groups.

P.M.   I see. Then what would you do?
L.C.   (1)_____ the various registers to (2)_____ when your parents married, (3)_____ their parents (4)_____, how many children they had.
P.M.   All this information (5)_____?
L.C.   Yes, (6)_____. There are birth certificates, death certificates, marriage certificates (7)_____.
P.M.   And (8)_____ for inspection?
L.C.   Yes, usually. Sometimes, (9)_____.

N   Writing activity

Listen to the interview again. List the points made by Laura Chapman and write a sentence about each of them.

O   Writing activity

Look again at exercise E on page 36. Imagine you are Mrs Piddock. Write a letter to your English friend, Mary Brown, describing what happened to you.

Summary

In this unit we practise using the *simple past* tense in contrast with the *past perfect*.

Example:
When she arrived at the checkout, she discovered that she *had lost* her purse.

Explain when we use the *simple past* and when we use the *past perfect*.

Remember that we use 'did' when asking questions in the *simple past*.

Example:
Why did she put her purse in the wire basket?
Did she lose all her money?

We also have further practice in using the *passive voice*, this time asking questions in the *present perfect* tense.

Example:
Has the missing purse been found yet?
Have the police been informed?

Note too a number of useful phrasal verbs with 'look':

to look after, to look for, to look out, to look forward to, to look into, to look through, to look up, to look in, to look round.

Give an example of somebody or something we might *look for* and somebody or something we might *look after*.

UNIT 6 The news

Reading activity

WHERE HAS ALL THE GOOD NEWS GONE?

1 What are your feelings as you watch the news on television? Is it just my
   imagination, or do the reports become a little more depressing every year?
   Floods in India, a drought in Africa, thousands starving in Asia, a bloody
   revolution in South America, a vicious murder in Peckham and forecasts of
5 the imminent collapse of the world's economy.

   Things didn't seem to be so bad when I was young. There were wars of course
   and I remember an earthquake or two. But in those days television was still a
   rich man's toy. We listened to the six o'clock news on
10 the radio. Perhaps reports of drought and famine have less impact when we
   hear about them on the radio than they do when accompanied by pictures of
   wretched cattle with their ribs sticking out and pathetic children with swollen
   bellies and hopeless eyes.

   To my grandfather, the future seemed full of promise. It was from newspapers
   that he learnt what was happening in the world. Communications were less
15 than perfect and it took a long time for details of any disaster to filter through
   to him. Plenty of dreadful things must have been taking place then too. But
   since the news-gathering services were not as efficient as they are today, the
   public heard far less about them.

20 Now of course communications are excellent. Television is all-powerful and the news services are adept at discovering and reporting sensational happenings in the most obscure corners of the world. Unfortunately, the most dramatic occurrences often tend to be disasters. So we are forced, in very self-defence, to become a little callous. Otherwise the burden of so much bad news would become intolerable.

A Questions

1 Where does the author suggest there may be too much water?
2 Where does he suggest there may be too little water?
3 Where does he suggest there may be a lot of hungry people?
4 What is the gloomy economic news to which he refers?
5 Why does the news seem 'worse' when it is brought to us on television?
6 Why didn't the writer watch television when he was a boy?
7 Why was it easier for the writer's grandfather to feel optimistic than it is for us today?
8 What effect does all the bad news have on people?

B Vocabulary exercise

1 Can you think of a job where plenty of *imagination* would be an asset? Explain why.
2 Can you think of a job where *too much imagination* might cause problems? Explain why.
3 If you lived in a two-storey house and the ground floor was *flooded*, how would you put things in order again once the flood had receded? Do you think you might have to throw anything away? Why?
4 Can you think of any part of the world where there has been a *drought* recently?
5 What are the results of a *famine*?
6 If you saw a young man with a *swollen* eye, what might you assume?
7 What do you think a *filter* might be made of? Can you think of any situations where it might be useful?
8 Can you think of any *dreadful* accidents that have occurred recently?
9 What would someone mean if they talked of an *obscure* writer or artist?

10 Why is there a danger of an ambulance-man or a policeman becoming *a little callous*?

C Vocabulary exercise

First find the words in italics in the reading passage. Then find two of the four words or phrases that could replace the italicised words *in this context*.

1 *reports* (line 2)
   a accounts
   b information
   c news
   d statements

2 *obscure* (line 21)
   a dark
   b vague
   c unknown
   d unfamiliar

3 *tend to* (line 22)
   a attend to
   b are inclined to
   c are apt to
   d move to

4 *disasters* (line 22)
   a mishaps
   b misfortunes
   c calamities
   d tragedies

5 *forced* (line 22)
   a obliged
   b ordered
   c compelled
   d commanded

6 *burden* (line 22)
   a obligation
   b load
   c responsibility
   d weight

D   Vocabulary exercise

Now try a word-study exercise. You will need your English-English Dictionary. Some of the key words are nouns, others are verbs or adjectives. The key words are in *italics*. Find the missing words in your dictionary and mark the syllable that should be stressed.

Here is an example: economy

Noun	Adjective	Verb	Adverb
e*con*omy	eco*nom*ical	e*con*omise	eco*nom*ically

Now you do it:

1 imagination
2 perfect
3 excel
4 force
5 defensive

E   Discussion

What were the main stories in the news? Make a list of them.

How many of the stories contain good news? How many contain bad news?

Why do you think so much bad news is reported?

Do you agree with the writer's conclusion?

F   Practice activity

Study this sentence

Plenty of dreadful things *must have been taking place* then too. (line 16)

We use 'must have been -ing' when we do not know for certain what was happening, but we can make a very good guess.

Example:
The murdered man was seated at his desk. In front of him was a pad of notepaper and a pen.
He must have been writing a letter.

Make more sentences using 'must have been':

1 The car crashed for no apparent reason. The driver was unconscious. Immediately the policeman opened the door he smelt alcohol. He said: _____.
2 When Robert and Geoffrey came to school, they both had black eyes and Robert had a cut lip. Their teacher said to another member of staff: _____.
3 Last year Henry played the accordion at the Christmas concert. He played very badly. This year he played the accordion again and performed very well. One of his colleagues said to another: _____
4 Jimmy was four years old. One night he woke up screaming in fright. His father rushed to his room and Jimmy said: 'There was a horrid man in my room.' Jimmy's father said: 'There's nobody here. You _____.'
5 The caretaker's flat was above the offices. One night he heard noises in the offices below. He rang the police. Thieves had broken in and escaped through a window. They had not stolen anything, but there were marks all round the lock of the safe. The caretaker said: _____

G   Practice activity

Study these ways of comparing things:

Communications are *better than* they used to be.
Fifty years ago communications were not *as good as* they are now.
People can communicate with one another *more easily than* they used to.
The news-gathering services are *much quicker* than they were 50 years ago.
Fifty years ago, the gathering of news was done *less quickly* than it is today.
I'm afraid the news is even *more depressing than* it was last night.
However, the news is *less depressing than* it was a week ago.

Here are some facts about Tom and his brother Harold. Compare them:

1 Harold is 43. His brother Tom is 38.
2 Harold works very hard. Tom doesn't work hard.
3 Harold is 5 feet 6 inches tall. Tom is 6 feet exactly.

4 Harold has a very interesting job. Tom has a boring job.
5 Harold has £10 000 in the bank. Tom has £100 in the bank.
6 Harold normally drives at 30 m.p.h. Tom usually drives at 40 m.p.h.
7 Harold is not a good driver. Tom drives very well.
8 Harold is overweight and takes little exercise. Tom is quite fit and plays tennis every week.

H Practice activity

You are planning to buy a watch to present to a colleague who is leaving your firm. You have looked at a lot of different watches and reduced the choice to six. Study the illustrations, compare the watches and choose one.

When comparing the watches, these words will be useful:

slim, heavy, ugly, modern, attractive, cheap, expensive, unusual, reliable, complicated.

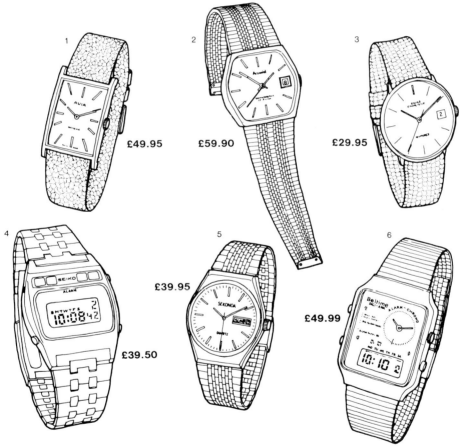

£49.95 £59.90 £29.95 £39.95 £39.50 £49.99

1	Avia	£49.95	17-jewel
2	Accurist	£59.90	17-jewel calendar
3	Swiss Emperor	£29.95	calendar
4	Seiko	£39.50	quartz alarm watch
5	Sekonda	£39.95	quartz day and date watch
6	Beltime	£49.99	quartz chiming alarm

We can make remarks like this:

I like the Avia.
Yes, I think it's *the most attractive*.
Do you? I think the Accurist is *more attractive than* the Avia.
The Beltime is definitely *the ugliest*.
Your taste is very old-fashioned.
I don't like the shape.

Dialogue 📼

Walter and Donald have been working in the City of London for six months. They met by chance at a Management Training Course, where they agreed that working in London was exciting, but a week of fresh air in Devon would be healthier. They are on a walking holiday at the moment, exploring Dartmoor.

Read the impression questions. Listen to the dialogue. Answer the questions and discuss your answers.

I Impression questions

a How do Donald and Walter feel about arriving in a town?

b Which of the two men do you think is fitter?

c How much have they had to eat during the day?

d Which of the two men is more interested in food, Walter or Donald?

e Do you think Walter buys a daily paper?

f Are Walter and Donald having an argument or a discussion?

g Which of the two opinions would you agree with, Walter's or Donald's.

h Is there any reason why Donald should buy two papers?

Now listen to the dialogue and follow the written instructions you have been given.

J Focus questions

In normal English conversation, we use many reference words, such as: it, they, that, you, there, he, etc.
Study this part of the dialogue, look at the words in *italics* (the reference words), listen and then say what you think these words refer to.

Here is an example:

DONALD	Television: *It* only scratches the surface.
	What does *it* refer to?

Now you do it:

| WALTER | I don't know what you mean by *that*. |
| **1** | What does *that* refer to? |

WALTER	The television pictures show you what happened and then the people concerned are interviewed and *they* tell you why it happened.
2	What does *they* refer to?
DONALD	*They* say what they saw.
3	What does *they* refer to?
WALTER	Yes, they are. They were *there*.
4	What does *there* refer to?
DONALD	*That* doesn't mean they're in a position to fill in the background.
5	What does *that* refer to?
DONALD	Anyway, the television pictures don't give *you* the whole truth.
6	What does *you* refer to?
DONALD	*They* only show you the bits that happened while the cameraman was filming.
7	What does *they* refer to?
DONALD	Very often, *he* missed the most important bits.
8	What does *he* refer to?
WAITRESS	Excuse me. I'm afraid *it's* almost half-past five.
9	What does *it's* refer to?
DONALD	See to *it*, will you, Walter?
10	What does *it* refer to?

K Discussion

Donald says that television only scratches the surface. Do you agree with him? Is he exaggerating?

How do *you* find out what is going on in the world? How much time do you spend each week:
a   reading newspapers,
b   watching television,
c   listening to the radio?

Donald and Walter didn't mention the radio, did they? Do you think the coverage of the news on the radio is good? How does it compare with the coverage on T.V. or in the newspapers?

Listening activity 📼

L Comprehension

Here are eight statements referring to the interview. Decide whether they are true or false.

1   A lot of the news printed in British newspapers isn't at all important.
2   Most people who buy British newspapers like to read the facts about what is happening in the world.
3   There are no really good newspapers in Britain.
4   Professor Hill's favourite newspaper doesn't always support the government.
5   If you read Professor Hill's favourite newspaper every day you would learn a lot about the latest films.
6   The sports writers who work for Professor Hill's favourite newspaper know their subject very well.
7   Several million copies of Professor Hill's favourite newspaper are sold every day.
8   People should be allowed to buy whatever sort of newspaper they want.

M Gap dictation

Professor Hill's lecture was rather controversial, and journalists who were attending the lecture asked him to repeat so that they could be quite sure their notes were accurate. Listen to the first half of Professor Hill's lecture again and write the phrases that are missing.

It seems to me that many British newspapers aren't really *news*papers (1) _____. They contain news, it is true, but (2) _____ only appears in print because

it is guaranteed to shock, surprise or cause a chuckle. What should we (3) _____ in a real newspaper? Interesting political articles? Accurate reports of (4) _____ in distant corners of the world? (5) _____ from the stock exchange? Full coverage of great sporting events? In-depth interviews with leading personalities? (6) _____ that in Britain the real newspapers, the ones that report the facts, sell in thousands, while the popular papers (7) _____ shock or amuse have a circulation of several million.

N Writing activity

Listen to the passage again. Here are some notes.

two kinds/ newspaper/ Britain
real newspapers/ facts/ popular newspapers/ entertain
British readers/ prefer
However/ wrong/ talk/ good/ bad/ newspapers/ aims/ different

Now write a paragraph about British newspapers using these notes.

O Writing activity

Do you have a favourite newspaper? What do you think makes a good newspaper?

Write a short description of the best newspaper in your country. Explain why you think it is the best.

UNIT 6   The news

Summary

In this unit we practise using the expression 'must have been -ing'.

Example:
Mr and Mrs Davis had been invited to tea by Mrs Clark.

When she saw the food laid out on the table, Mrs Davis said: 'My goodness, you must have been working for hours.'

Explain when we use the 'must-have-been-ing' construction.

We also revise comparatives:
Example: His is a *faster* car than mine.

and superlatives:

Example:
It's the *most ridiculous* suggestion I've ever heard.

What is the comparative and superlative of:
big, busy, pretty and interesting?

What is the comparative and superlative of the adjectives:
good, bad, little, far and old (used for people)?

What is the comparative and superlative of the adverbs:
slowly, happily, hard, well and badly?

UNIT 7   Crime and punishment

Reading activity

THE SILVER SHADOW

1   Life was never easy for Alec McBain. He was born in a poor area of Glasgow,
his father was killed in an accident when he was four and a year later his
mother died. Alec and his two brothers were put in an orphanage.

    One day the orphanage children were taken on an outing to visit Edinburgh
5   Castle. That was the day Alec fell in love with the silver Rolls Royce. It was
parked outside the entrance to the Castle and when he saw it, Alec's eyes
nearly popped out of his head.

    'Have you ever seen such a fine car?' he cried, 'One day I'm going to buy my-
self one like that.'
10 Miss McKinney, who was in charge of the party, smiled.
    'You'll have to work very hard and earn a lot of money to buy a car like that,'
she said.
    'Oh, I'll work hard, Miss,' replied Alec, his eyes shining.

    At sixteen, Alec left the orphanage and found a job on a building site. As soon
15 as he was eighteen, he enlisted in the army. He came out of the army in 1973
and for four years he endured the tough, dreary life on a North Sea oil rig.
Then he spent two years working in Saudi Arabia. And all this time he never
forgot the Rolls Royce. The thought of owning one became a kind of
obsession, a dream that sustained him through dangerous night patrols in
20 Northern Ireland, through bitterly cold winter days on the oil rig and through
the sweltering heat of a Saudi Arabian summer.

But month by month the money in his bank account increased, until at last his dream came true and he drove out of a London showroom in his own gleaming Rolls Royce Silver Shadow. It was almost new and it cost him £20 000,
25 paid in cash.

By this time, he had bought himself a small bachelor flat in south London and the silver Rolls Royce soon became a familiar sight standing in front of the house. One Sunday he decided to drive down to the coast. He reached Brighton about eleven and he was cruising slowly along a narrow street look-
30 ing for somewhere to park, when he saw a group of youths coming towards him, some walking on the pavement and some in the road.

Everything then happened very quickly. One of the youths claimed that the Rolls hit him as it went by. Swearing and cursing they began kicking the car. McBain, wild with fury, leapt out of the car, grabbed a heavy spanner from the
35 boot and attacked them. Three were injured and the others fled. The police were quickly on the scene and McBain was arrested. He denied hitting anyone with the Rolls, but pleaded guilty to assault. He said the youths were jealous because he owned a prestige car. The repairs to the bodywork will cost £1200.

A Questions

1 In what way was Alec McBain's upbringing different from that of most children?
2 What were the two tragedies that affected him when he was young?
3 What was Alec doing at Edinburgh Castle?
4 What was Miss McKinney's connection with Alec?
5 We don't know where Alec McBain works now. But when he applied for his present post he was asked to give details of 'previous employment'. Where did Alec spend some of his time when he was a soldier?
6 Why did McBain drive down the narrow street?
7 Why do *you* think the youths attacked his car?
8 Why did the youths run away?

B Vocabulary exercise

1 Can you think of any *areas* in the world where there is a shortage of water? Name some.
2 Think of some reasons why the police might temporarily close an *area* of a city to the public.
3 When did you last go on an *outing*? Where did you go? What did you do?
4 Note the expression: '*Alec's eyes nearly popped out of his head*'. (line 6) Can you think of an occasion when your eyes nearly popped out of your head?

5 Why might life on a North Sea oil rig be (a) *dreary*, (b) *tough*?
6 Think of some more ambitions that might become '*a kind of obsession*' for the person concerned.
7 Can you think of any jobs where men might have to work in '*sweltering heat*'?
8 A *gleaming* Rolls Royce is a highly polished Rolls Royce. What other things might we describe as gleaming?
9 Three of the youths were *injured* by McBain. There are many ways of getting injured. Can you think of one or two unusual ones?
10 McBain said the youths were *jealous* of his car. Think of one or two more situations in which somebody might become jealous.

C Vocabulary exercise

Here are six sentences from the reading passage. After each sentence, you will find four sentences which have more or less the same meaning. Choose the *one* sentence that is closest to the original meaning.

1 Alec and his two brothers were put in an orphanage.
   a Alec and his two brothers were established in an orphanage.
   b Alec and his two brothers were set up in an orphanage.

c Alec and his two brothers were sent to an orphanage.
d Alec and his brothers were ordered to an orphanage.

2 One day the orphanage children were taken on an outing.
   a One day the orphanage children were taken on a holiday.
   b One day the orphanage children were taken on a cruise.
   c One day the orphanage children were taken on a voyage.
   d One day the orphanage children were taken on a day trip.

3 As soon as he was 18, he enlisted in the army.
   a As soon as he was 18, he joined the army.
   b As soon as he was 18, he was conscripted into the army.
   c As soon as he was 18, he was drafted into the army.
   d As soon as he was 18, he was allowed into the army.

4 He came out of the army in 1973.
   a He retired from the army in 1973.
   b He deserted the army in 1973.
   c He left the army in 1973.
   d He escaped from the army in 1973..

5 For four years he endured the tough, dreary life on a North Sea oil rig.
   a For four years he stood the tough, dreary life on a North Sea oil rig.
   b For four years he managed the tough, dreary life on a North Sea oil rig.
   c For four years he tolerated the tough, dreary life on a North Sea oil rig.
   d For four years he encountered the tough, dreary life on a North Sea oil rig.

6 Month by month the money in his bank account increased.
   a Month by month the money in his bank account developed.
   b Month by month the money in his bank account enlarged.
   c Month by month the money in his bank account profited.
   d Month by month the money in his bank account grew.

D Discussion

McBain appeared in the Magistrate's court. The magistrates could:
a Send him to prison for three months.
b Fine him anything from £20 to £100.
c Give him a conditional discharge (in which case he would go free, but if he committed another crime, this assault would be taken into consideration when he was sentenced).

If you were the magistrates, what would your sentence be?

E Practice activity

Alec enjoyed talking to Miss McKinney. On the bus back to the orphanage, he sat beside her and they continued their conversation:

MISS McK.	What are you going to do when you grow up then?
ALEC	I don't know. I think maybe I'll join the army.
MISS McK.	Oh, you'll look very smart in your uniform.
ALEC	Do soldiers earn a lot of money?
MISS McK.	Officers do.
ALEC	But I'm sure they won't make me an officer.
MISS McK.	They won't at first.
ALEC	I think I'd have to go to one of those posh schools if I wanted to become an officer.
MISS McK.	No, you can join as an ordinary soldier and apply to become an officer later on.
ALEC	I don't think I'll join the army, after all. I think I'll work in a circus instead. Do lion-tamers earn a lot of money?
MISS McK.	I'm not sure. They probably do.
ALEC	But lions are a bit dangerous, aren't they? I think I'm going to be a clown in a circus and squirt water all over the other clowns ...

When they got back to the orphanage Miss McKinney had tea with some of the other members of the orphanage staff. She told them about her conversation with Alec.

Alec said: 'One day I'm going to buy myself one like that.'
Miss McKinney said: He said that one day *he was going* to buy himself one like that.

UNIT 7   Crime and punishment

Miss McKinney said to Alec: 'You'll have to work very hard and earn a lot of money.'

She said to the staff: I told him *he would have to* work very hard and earn a lot of money.

Continue Miss McKinney's account of the conversation:
Note: 'Don't', 'Didn't' etc count as one word.

MISS McK. I asked him what he _____ when he _____ up. Alec said he _____ know. He _____ maybe he _____ the army. So I told him he _____ look very smart in his uniform. He asked if soldiers _____ a lot of money. I said that officers _____. Alec said he _____ sure they _____ him an officer and I agreed that they _____ at first. Alec said he _____ he'd have to go to one of those posh schools if he wanted to become an officer. But I told him that he _____ as an ordinary soldier and apply to become an officer later on. He said he _____ he _____ join the army after all. He _____ he _____ in a circus instead. Then he asked if lion tamers _____ a lot of money. I said I _____ sure. They probably _____. Then it occurred to him that lions _____ a bit dangerous. So finally he decided he _____ going to be a clown in a circus and squirt water all over the other clowns . . .

F   Practice activity

Note these two examples of verbs followed by the gerund:

They began kicking the car. (line 33)
He denied hitting anyone. (line 36)

Here is a list of useful verbs which are followed by the gerund:

avoid, can't bear, deny, delay, enjoy, forgive, finish, it's no use, keep, mind, prevent, risk, stop, suggest and the adjective 'worth'.

Add a suitable expression from the list above and one word of your own to complete the following sentences:
1 It's probably w__ __ to the airline office in person. They'll have all the information there.
2 Oh, not another queue. I c_____ b__ __ in queues.
3 F_____ my _____ you so late, but there's something I must talk to you about.
4 I always try to a__ __ the shopping at the weekend. The shops get so crowded.
5 I must say I e__ __ Daniel's home movies. Wasn't that sequence with the elephants hilarious?
6 Her d__ __ her till the last possible moment, because he knew she'd be furious.
7 He d_____ ever _____ to the girl, but I know he's lying.
8 Excuse me. I can't get past. Would you m__ __ your suitcase, please.
9 He didn't trip Jordan up, but he p_____ him from _____ the ball, so it's an indirect free kick.
10 Have you f__ __ my typewriter? I need it.
11 We can't r__ __ him go now. He knows too much.
12 I'm sorry we're out of stock of the book. I s__ __ at the library if they have a copy.
13 It's no u__ __ Dan. He never knows anything.
14 She's sleeping better now. Thank goodness she's s__ __ those awful dreams.
15 What's wrong with your watch? I don't know exactly. It k__ __.

Dialogue oo

Before you listen to the dialogue, study the Impression questions. You will then know what to concentrate on while you are listening. Here is the background:
Mr and Mrs Carstairs live in a quiet, respectable suburb. At the moment, Mr Carstairs is watching the 9 o'clock news and Mrs Carstairs is knitting.

G   Impression questions

a   How old do you think the Carstairs are?
b   Is Emma friendly with Henry?
c   Why does Henry want to have a word with Emma in private?
d   What does James Carstairs think of Henry McCarthy?
e   Who do you think Martha is?
f   What is the problem with Martha?

Crime and punishment   UNIT 7

g What sort of things has Martha been 'accumulating'?
h What is going to happen to her?
g How would you describe James Carstairs?
h Do you agree with James Carstairs' last remark?

Now listen to the dialogue. Tell your teacher if you would like to listen to all or part of it again.

H   Focus questions

It is the morning after the telephone conversation. Emma Carstairs is visiting Martha McCarthy. Imagine that you are Emma and talk to Martha. Here is an example:
EMMA   How are you feeling today, Martha?
MARTHA   I'm feeling weak . . . and I have a terrible headache.

Now you do it:

1 EMMA   _____
       MARTHA   I don't know whether he's coming this morning or this afternoon. Doctors are so busy these days.

2 EMMA   _____
       MARTHA   No, I haven't been feeling hungry recently.

3 EMMA   _____
       MARTHA   Thank you, I'd love one. The medicine has made me so thirsty.

4 EMMA   _____
       MARTHA   Not really. Could you fetch another blanket from the cupboard?

5 EMMA   _____
       MARTHA   If you can spare the time, Emma, I'd love to see you this afternoon.

I   Discussion

Mr Carstairs obviously thinks that Martha deserves to be sent to prison. Do you?

From the information you have heard, why do you believe that Martha has been shoplifting?

Is shoplifting a problem in your country?

Are the people who are caught shoplifting usually very poor? Why do you think people who are not very poor sometimes steal things from shops?

Listening activity 📼

J   Comprehension

Here are eight statements referring to the conversation between Robert and Muriel. Say whether they are true or false:

1 Robert thinks that the two young men who attacked the old lady got very severe sentences.
2 Both the young men were sent to prison.
3 Muriel read about a man who killed a little boy.
4 She thinks the man responsible was punished too lightly.
5 During the conversation Muriel reminds Robert about something he had forgotten.
6 A railway employee was injured in the Great Train Robbery.
7 The Great Train Robbers didn't manage to steal a lot of money.
8 Muriel thinks you should get a heavier punishment for injuring people than you should for stealing.

K   Gap dictation

The listening comprehension is fairly short, but there are a lot of important and useful phrases and words. Before you listen again, study the gaps and try to imagine and remember the words that were used. This time there will be more help for you because there will be a gap for every missing word.

ROBERT   The sentences (1)_____ _____ for crimes of violence.
MURIEL   What particular case are you talking about?
ROBERT   (2)_____ _____ _____ _____ _____. These two young men (3)_____ _____ an old lady's flat, tied her up, forced her to tell them (4)_____ _____ _____ _____ _____. Left her with a broken nose, a broken arm and bruises (5)_____ _____ _____ _____. Stole her life

53

savings; (6)£_____ _____ _____
_____ _____ _____ _____?

MURIEL   What *did* they get?

ROBERT   (7)_____ was sent to prison for three months; (8)_____ _____ got a conditional discharge.

L   Writing activity

Listen to the conversation again and write a short summary of Robert and Muriel's ideas.

M   Writing activity

Below is a list of crimes and the sentences imposed by the courts. Study them:

Category of crime	Brief details	Sentence
Robbery with violence	A sub-postmaster was threatened with a gun by two men. They hit him over the head and stole £5000. Both men had been to prison previously.	Both got eight years in prison.
Wounding	A man was stabbed outside a pub after an argument. The attacker had no criminal record.	He was conditionally discharged.
Murder	A baby boy was attacked on a number of occasions by his stepfather. Finally the stepfather killed the child.	The stepfather got three years in prison.
Fraud	A 53-year-old businessman persuaded a number of people to invest £200 000 in a mining company. In fact the mine did not exist and the investors lost their money.	He got 12 years in prison.
Dangerous driving	A man driving while under the influence of alcohol ran into a motor scooter and badly injured the two riders. One young man lost a leg as a result of the accident.	The driver got two years in prison and was banned from driving for 10 years.

Now write a letter to a newspaper, using about 200 words, giving your views on crime and punishment today.

Summary

In this unit we practise turning future statements into *reported speech*.

Example:
John: 'I'll get one for you.'
John said he would (he'd) get one for me.
Sue: 'I'm going to telephone her on Tuesday.'
Sue said she was going to telephone her on Tuesday.

What changes do we make in future tenses when direct speech becomes indirect speech?

In addition, note the useful verbs listed in Practice activity F which are followed by the gerund.

Examples:
He couldn't *avoid hitting* the bicycle.
She *risked losing* her job to get him the information.
He *delayed giving* her the news till the next morning.

UNIT 8   It's all in the mind

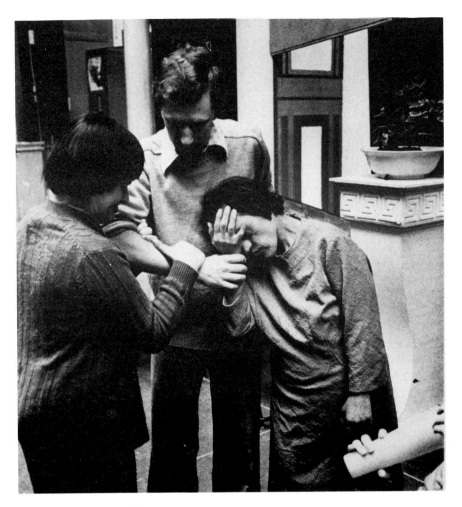

Reading activity

I'M NOT CRAZY, DOCTOR . . .

1   A disturbing report appeared recently in the magazine *Science*. The report
describes an experiment, the results of which suggest that there are occasions
when psychiatrists have great difficulty in distinguishing between people who
are mentally disturbed and those who are sane.

5   In the course of the experiment, eight perfectly normal people gained
admission to psychiatric wards in a number of different hospitals. They all
complained of hearing voices repeating the words 'empty', 'hollow' and
'thud'.

The eight fake patients included several trained doctors, who lied about their
10 occupation. They also lied about their names and naturally about their
symptoms. But in all other respects they told the truth concerning their lives
and their personal relationships; and once they had been admitted to hospital
they behaved quite normally.

15 However, as soon as they had been officially labelled 'mentally ill', everything they did tended to confirm the diagnosis in the eyes of the medical staff. For instance, if one of the 'patients' approached a doctor and asked a perfectly sensible question such as 'Pardon me doctor, could you tell me when I will be allowed to use the tennis courts?', the doctor's normal response was to walk straight on, ignoring the question.

20 On the other hand, the real patients inside the institution were not nearly so easy to convince. 'You're not crazy. You're checking up on the hospital,' was a typical comment.

The eight fake patients stayed in the mental institutions for periods of from seven to 52 days. One is forced to the frightening conclusion that once a
25 person has disappeared behind the walls of a mental institution, it may prove extremely difficult to convince the medical authorities that he or she is not in fact mentally ill.

A Questions

1 Explain exactly why the eight normal people went into hospital.
2 Why did they not all go to the same hospital?
3 How truthful were the eight 'patients' when they entered the hospitals?
4 How did the eight patients show they were 'crazy'?
5 Why do you think the doctors tended to ignore questions such as 'Could you tell me when I will be allowed to use the tennis court'?
6 Why does the writer consider the result of the experiment frightening?

B Vocabulary exercise

1 This report is about mental illness. Think of another aspect of society today about which a committee might issue *a disturbing report*.
2 Do you know what sort of *experiments* are carried out on animals? Why is this done?
3 All doctors must sometimes have difficulty in *distinguishing between* one illness and another. Give any examples you can think of.
4 The opposite of *sane* is insane. You are watching a rather melodramatic film. One character says to another 'You can't do it. You must be insane.' Suggest what the second character might be intending to do.
5 The opposite of *hollow* is solid. Think of some sports equipment which is hollow and some which is solid.

6 The word *fake* is sometimes used about art or jewellery. Why might a rich man be cross if you used it about something he had bought? What might he have bought?
7 The *symptoms* of a disease or illness are the clues that tell the doctor what is wrong with the patient. Do you know what the symptoms are for any common illnesses?
8 John Hudson is a successful businessman, happily married with two children. Twenty years ago he did something stupid and went to jail. His family know nothing of this. Now someone is trying to blackmail him. What is the only *sensible* thing to do?
9 The people came off the cross-Channel ferry at Dover and passed through the Customs Hall. When John Smith came though, the customs men *ignored* him. Why?
10 How can a class teacher *check up* on the progress of his students?

C Vocabulary exercise

In these seven pairs of word problems, one key word is used in each of the sentences in the pairs. However, the meaning of the key word is different. All the key words are taken from the reading passage.
Here is what you should do: Find the key word in the word problem pairs. Find the key word in the reading passage and decide what it means. Explain the different meanings in the problem pairs.

1 You were crazy to drive so fast.
I'm crazy about hang-gliding.

2 Professor Hanson is distinguishing himself in the field of nuclear energy.
His distinguishing features are his very long nose and large ears.

3 Your behaviour was perfectly disgusting. Why did you hit him?
My secretary has managed to reproduce this document perfectly.

4 Admission to British museums is usually free.
The court was amazed by the accused's admission of guilt.

5 Gertrude is such a snob. She never behaves naturally.
Tropical plants do not grow naturally in Britain.

6 I wonder if I could make a personal call.
Personal remarks are not suitable in a discussion.

7 I've only been to Japan once.
I'm angry because you never once offered to help.

D Discussion

Do you think it was fair on the doctors who worked in the hospitals to carry out this experiment? Would you be prepared to take part in an experiment like this? If so, what might scare you?

What action would you take if you were a doctor and you suspected that one of your patients was not really ill?

Why do you think it was that the fake patients found it easier to fool the doctors than the other patients?

E Practice activity

Note this example of a verb followed by the gerund:

They all *complained of hearing* voices repeating the words 'empty', 'hollow' and 'thud'. (line 6)

Here is a list of some more verbs which are followed by the gerund:

catch, can't help, dread, detest, excuse, fancy, imagine, look forward to, postpone, remember, resent, try (experiment), understand, and the expression 'it's no good'.

Add a suitable expression from the list above and one word of your own to complete the following sentences. If necessary, use your dictionary:

1 I'm thirsty. Do you f____ ____ for a cup of coffee?
2 Simon hated the job. He only had a week's holiday and he d____ ____ back to work.
3 I know I learn slowly, but I r____ your ____ that I'm lazy.
4 I think we'd better p____ ____ a decision about the appointment till you get back from Brussels.
5 Right, see you on Friday, and tell your wife I'm l____ f____ very much to ____ her.
6 Please e____ my ____ but are those diamonds real?
7 I can't get this stain out. Why don't you t____ ____ it in detergent?
8 It's n____ g____ ____ me because you can't find your passport.
9 I can't u____ your not ____ to come to the party.
10 I r____ ____ him speak at a meeting many years ago.

F Practice activity

Study these extracts from the Reading activity:

A disturbing report appeared *recently* . . . (line 1)
. . . eight *perfectly* normal people (line 5)
. . . and *naturally* about their symptoms (line 10)
. . . they behaved *quite normally* (line 13)
. . . it may prove *extremely* difficult . . . (line 25)

All the words in *italics* are adverbs. This exercise will give you a chance to check that you are using some of the most useful adverbs correctly. Which expressions (a, b, c, d) could be used to complete the sentence? (Note: More than one expression may be correct.)

1 The doctors work ____.
a hardly
b extremely
c hard
d barely

2 That patient plays the piano ____.
a well
b good
c badly
d bad

3 I have _____ any money.
   a almost
   b scarcely
   c barely
   d nearly

4 She has _____ no money.
   a almost
   b practically
   c hardly
   d scarcely

5 He asked the doctor a _____ sensible question.
   a perfectly
   b nearly
   c very
   d rather

6 Some of the patients behave _____.
   a strangely
   b normally
   c unusual
   d bad

7 They were playing tennis_____.
   a happy
   b well
   c friendly
   d enthusiastic

8 The story he told was _____ true.
   a absolutely
   b unfortunately
   c badly
   d likely

9 The young doctor talked to the patients _____.
   a slowly
   b friendly
   c lovely
   d nicely

10 The nurses treated the patients _____.
   a fair
   b kindly
   c well
   d good

G   Practice activity

The position of adverbs is a little complicated in English. This exercise is designed to provide practice in finding the places where adverbs can be used, and explore the changes in meaning that may result.

After each sentence there is an adverb. Decide where we could put the adverb in the sentence. Remember that adverbs can sometimes be used in more than one position.

Example:
I *recently* saw a report in the magazine *Science*.
I saw a report *recently* in the magazine *Science*.
Recently I saw a report in the magazine *Science*.
I saw a report in the magazine *Science recently*.

Now you do it:

1 She speaks Greek. (fluently)
2 I told the doctor about it. (naturally)
3 I don't eat breakfast. (fast)
4 He got into the house. (easily)
5 It was difficult to get a ticket. (extremely)
6 I'm going to ask him about the programme. (tomorrow)
7 He told me he hated his job. (once)
8 They have arguments. (often)
9 It was a long journey. (fairly)
10 He hasn't given me the money. (still)
11 I wrote to the firm. (yesterday)
12 She typed the letter. (beautifully)

It's all in the mind

GROUND FLOOR
Plastic toys
Assembly kits
Educational toys

FIRST FLOOR
Toys for 6-18months

SECOND FLOOR
Electronics, TV games
Telecommunications

THIRD FLOOR
Dolls, dolls' houses
Large, woolly animals

FOURTH FLOOR
Electric trains
Automated cars, boats
and planes. Toy soldiers

Dialogue 📼

H   Impression questions

Terry and Alison work in a specialist department store in London. Many of Terry's customers are middle-aged men. A lot of Alison's customers have just become grandmothers.

Look at the photographs and read the introduction. Then say what you *think* are the answers to these questions.

1   What kind of department store do Terry and Alison work in?
2   Which department does Alison work in?
3   Which floor does Terry work on?
4   What age group does the second floor cater for?
5   What age group does the third floor cater for?

Discuss your answers with other members of the class. They may ask you for reasons.

I   Impression questions

Listen to Terry and Alison. They are having a quick snack in the employees' canteen. After you have listened, answer the Impression questions.

1   Do you think Alison and Terry have the same feelings about men who play war games?
2   What words would you use to describe Terry's impression?
3   How would you describe Alison's attitude?
4   Why does Alison disapprove of the toys she sells?
5   Terry and Alison use the word 'normal'. What is the difference in meaning in the way they use the word?

J   Focus questions

Because Terry and Alison work in the same situation and know one another, they use a great many idiomatic expressions. Remember that Terry said, 'It's *lovely* to have a little peace and quiet.' In another situation, Terry might use 'lovely' to describe the same feeling. He could say: 'It's lovely to have a holiday.'

Now use the idiomatic expressions in italics with the same meaning, in other contexts:

1 TERRY 'There are some funny people *about*.'
YOU _____

2 TERRY '*I've no idea* what people buy for girls.'
YOU _____

3 ALISON 'It's not *really* quiet, but the noises are different.'
YOU _____

4 ALISON 'Certainly not. They're too busy doing *the real thing*.'
YOU _____

5 ALISON '*At least* it's a better idea than a singing teddy bear.'
YOU _____

K Discussion

Terry is critical of grown men who play with toys. Are you?

Alison is critical of war games. Are you?

Alison is critical of sophisticated toys. Are you?

Alison wonders what the word 'normal' means. What do you think it means? Is it normal for boys to play with guns and girls to play with dolls?

Listening activity 📼

L Comprehension

Here are eight statements referring to James and Susan's discussion. Decide whether they are true or false.

1 Hancock made people laugh.
2 Hancock worked on radio and television.
3 Galton and Simpson were actors who worked with Hancock.
4 Hancock wasn't an easy man to work with.
5 Hancock committed suicide.
6 Hancock divorced his wife.
7 Hancock took a lot of pills.
8 Not many people find Hancock amusing today.

M Gap dictation

Listen again to a part of the Listening comprehension and fill in the missing words or groups of words.

SUSAN 'What (1)_____ _____?'
JAMES 'Well, he was (2)_____ _____ _____ his own performance.'
JAMES 'If you listened to the radio shows regularly, you (3)_____ _____ _____ _____ a real person.'
JAMES 'He (4)_____ _____ _____ an international star.'
JAMES 'He (5)_____ all the people (6)_____ _____ _____, including Galton and Simpson.'

SUSAN 'And you can listen to those old radio shows today and (7)_____ _____ _____ as they were twenty years ago.'
JAMES (8)_____ _____. He was a very great comedian. (9)_____ _____ _____ _____ _____.'

It's all in the mind

N   Writing activity

Listen to the discussion again. List the points made about the real Hancock by Susan and James. Write complete sentences.

O   Writing activity

In Hancock's case, the very aspects of his personality that made him a great comedian probably made him a difficult man to work with.

Name some other famous person who must have been difficult to work with and explain why. You will need 150–200 words.

Summary

In this unit we note a further group of useful verbs which are followed by the gerund. They are listed in Practice activity E.

Examples:
I *fancy going* for a walk. Do you?
It's *no good asking* me to explain.

Then we practise using adverbs:

I understand *perfectly*.
He nodded *slowly*. 'I think you're right,' he said.
She *recently* returned from a visit to Alaska.
The picnic was a marvellous idea, but *unfortunately* it poured with rain all day.

It is sometimes difficult to know exactly where to place adverbs in English. Here are some examples to note:

She speaks English *fluently*.
He spoke *kindly* to the young girl.
He came to the office *yesterday*.
He *still* hasn't finished speaking.
Have you visited the museum *yet*?
I *seldom* travel on public transport.
Howard played *well*, but he should have saved that third goal.

Could any of the adverbs in the sentences above be placed in different positions? If they were, how would it affect the meaning of the sentence?

UNIT 9   It's not good enough!

Delicious!

Reading activity

WILLIAM

1   It was a cold, unfriendly day in early December. I hurried into the sweetshop
beside the bus stop and bought a bar of chocolate. The bus arrived, I climbed
in and sat down. I turned the chocolate over and read the notice on the back.
'We want this chocolate to reach you in perfect condition. If you have any
5   complaint, please return the chocolate, with the wrapper and the name of the
store where you purchased it . . .', and I thought of William.

I am not a complainer. If I go to a restaurant where the soup is cold and the
waiters are rude, I do not call for the manager and complain. I just don't go to
that restaurant again; but William is different. I called on him one Sunday
10   morning when he was turning out his desk and he showed me a whole
collection of letters from unfortunate manufacturers whose products he had
complained about.

One day he bought an apple pie. The picture on the outside of the packet
showed a pie, cut in half, and filled with fruit. William was not happy that this
15   illustration reflected the true state of affairs. 'The quality of your pies used to
be excellent,' he wrote, 'but you have obviously decided to economise by
cutting down on the amount of fruit you put in your products. On opening the
apple pie in question, I found that it was approximately half full of fruit. I am
therefore of the opinion that your illustration was totally misleading . . . ' The
20   manufacturer sent William a selection of his products, trusting William
would find them to his satisfaction.

William bought a jar of strawberry jam. He counted the strawberries and found there were eleven. 'Your television advertisements state that your jam is packed with fruit,' he wrote. 'Eleven strawberries in a jar could in no way be
25 described as packed with fruit.' The firm sent him half-a-dozen different varieties of their jam and requested his comments.

William has complained that sausages contained too much pepper, that the tobacco in cigarettes was a funny colour, that scones were stale and that tinned salmon had a funny smell. A week ago he bought a beautiful fruit cake,
30 crammed tight with cherries and nuts and raisins. Unfortunately, there was a small stone in the first slice he sampled and he broke a front tooth.

The dentist tells him he can't have it done under the National Health so it's going to cost him £80. He has written to the manufacturer with the stone stuck to the top of the letter with sticky tape.
35 'Do you think I should have included the broken tooth?' he asked me anxiously.
'I'm sure that wasn't necessary,' I told him. 'They'll believe you.'

A Questions

1 What is a customer told to do if he is dissatisfied with the chocolate?
2 How does the writer differ from William?
3 Can you explain how William obtained so many letters from different firms?
4 What was wrong with the apple pie?
5 What was his complaint about the strawberries?
6 Was it worth his while complaining about the strawberries? Give reasons for your answer.
7 Explain how William broke his tooth.
8 What was it that still worried William after he had written to the manufacturer of the cake?

B Vocabulary exercise

1 William returned the chocolate with the *wrapper*. What might you wrap round a parcel before you post it?
2 Waiters can be *rude*; so can shop assistants. How might a shop assistant be rude?
3 Name some products that are *manufactured* in your country.
4 When a motorist buys a new car, he often examines it very critically. What might he *find fault* with?
5 Advertisements are not supposed to be *misleading*, but they aften are. Can you think of some?

6 What might a *jam-jar* be used for after you have eaten all the jam?
7 What different *varieties* of jam can you think of?
8 Scones can be *stale*. What else might go stale if you keep it too long?
9 The cake was *crammed tight* with fruit and nuts. When might a suitcase be crammed tight?
10 What kind of things are people sometimes invited to *sample* in a big store?

C Vocabulary exercise

First you will read a sentence taken from the reading passage, with the key word in *italics*. Study the key word and the way it is used. Then use the key word in another form and write your own sentence – any sentence you like so long as you follow the instructions.

Example:
'It was a *cold*, unfriendly day.'
(Use an adverb) The manager looked at me coldly.

Now you do it:
1 Example: 'We want these chocolates to reach you in *perfect* condition.' (Use an adverb.)
2 Example: 'The bus *arrived*. (Use a noun.)
3 Example: 'If you have any *complaint*, please return the wrapper.' (Use a verb.)

4   Example: 'I am of the opinion that your illustration was *totally* misleading.'
(Use a noun.)

5   Example: 'There was a small stone in the first slice he *sampled*.'
(Use a noun.)

6   Example: 'The manufacturer sent William a selection of his *products*.'
(Use a verb.)

7   Example: 'Do you think I should have included the broken tooth?' he asked me *anxiously*.
(Use an adjective.)

8   Example: 'The manufacturer trusted that William would find them to his *satisfaction*.'
(Use an adjective.)

D   Discussion

Think carefully. What have you complained about in a shop or restaurant or café recently?

If you were the manager of a restaurant, you would have to deal with customers' complaints. What sort of things do you think customers might complain about?

Have you ever found it necessary to complain about anything you bought? Explain what happened.

How much sympathy do you have with William? Do you consider him:

a   a public-spirited citizen, determined to keep up standards?

b   a rather silly person who is always looking for reasons to complain about things?

E   Practice activity

One day William bought a blue pullover. When he washed it, it shrank. So naturally he took it back to the shop.

ASSISTANT	Good morning, sir. Can I help you?
WILLIAM	Yes, I want to change this pullover. I bought it three weeks ago, and I'm afraid it's not satisfactory.
ASSISTANT	I'm sorry about that, sir. What's the trouble?
WILLIAM	Well, when I washed it, it shrank. Look at it. I can't wear that.
ASSISTANT	Did you follow the washing instructions on the label, sir?
WILLIAM	Yes, of course I did.

ASSISTANT	They're pure wool, you see, sir, and if you wash them in hot water, they *will* shrink.
WILLIAM	I followed the instructions exactly. I only used soap flakes and warm water and I dried it on the clothes line in the garden.
ASSISTANT	I see, sir. I'll have a word with the manager.

Imagine you bought a pink shirt. When you washed it the colour 'ran' – that is, the colour came out and made the rest of your washing pink. You take it back to the shop. Complete the conversation:

ASSISTANT	Good morning, can I help you?
YOU	Yes, _____.
ASSISTANT	I'm sorry about that. What's the trouble?
YOU	Well, _____.
ASSISTANT	Did you follow the washing instructions on the label?
YOU	Yes, _____.
ASSISTANT	Sometimes the colour runs a little bit the first time you wash them, but you shouldn't have any more trouble with it.
YOU	_____.
ASSISTANT	I see. I'll have a word with the manager.

Practise complaining about things you have bought, which were not satisfactory:

1   A red blouse. The colour ran when you washed it.

2   An electric clock. It keeps stopping.

3   A cassette recorder. It won't record.

4   A radio. The sound quality is very bad.

5   A toaster. Always burns the toast.

F   Practice activity

William asked this question:

'Do you think I *should have included* the broken tooth?' (line 35)

Now here are some more situations. What *should* or *shouldn't* William *have done*?

1   William was trying to repair his television set while it was still plugged into the mains. He got a shock.

It's not good enough! UNIT 9

2 William was late for his appointment at the dentist's. He didn't telephone, he didn't change his appointment. He went straight round to the dentist's surgery, but the dentist refused to see him.

3 William stood at the bus stop waiting for the bus. It began to rain and William got very wet.

4 William was driving along the motorway when they passed a petrol station. 'Don't you think we should fill up with petrol?' suggested his friend, Jimmy. 'Oh, there's plenty in the tank,' said William. Soon afterwards they ran out of petrol.

5 William was sometimes rather outspoken. One day he said to his boss: 'I think that's a very foolish decision.' 'If you do,' replied his boss, 'then I think you'd better find yourself another job.'

6 William was always on the lookout for a bargain. He bought a second-hand radio. He didn't pay much for it, but it never worked well.

7 William was in a hurry. He was driving towards the traffic lights when they changed to red. He drove straight on. He didn't realise there was a police car behind him.

8 William got into an argument with a very large lorry driver in a motorway cafe. 'What did you call me, son?' asked the lorry driver. William said it again and the lorry driver hit him.

G Practice activity

Note these phrases from the Reading activity:

. . . one Sunday morning when he was *turning out* his desk . . . (line 9)
. . . by *cutting down on* the amount of fruit you put in your products. (line 16)

The verbs 'turn' and 'cut' are frequently used with prepositions and adverbs. For example:

I asked her to *turn down* the volume on that record-player but she *turned* it *up*.
She *turned on* the light; he *turned off* the radio.
A lot of people were *turned away from* the concert because all the tickets had been sold.
First you toast the bun on one side; then you *turn it over*.
We *turned out* the shed at the bottom of the garden and found some extraordinary things.
She promised to *cut down on* her smoking.
When the snow fell, the farm was *cut off* for nearly a week.
Right, let's *cut out* the fooling about and get some work done.

Replace the words in italics by suitable expressions with 'turn' or 'cut'. Use each expression once only.
1 We were *refused admission to* the dance, because we didn't have tickets.
2 Why did they *remove* that scene from the film?
3 Where did you get those roller skates? I found them when I was *tidying* the garage.
4 I asked him to *reduce* the volume on his radio, but he refused, so I hit him.
5 I'm afraid we're going to have to *reduce* the number of temporary staff we take on at Christmas-time.

Dialogue 📼

Roger Hart booked into the Regal Hotel at 4 o'clock. He was given the key to room number 43 and told it was on the third floor. It is now 4.30 and Roger has Returned to reception. Before you listen to the dialogue, study the Impression questions.

H Impression questions
1 How many complaints did you hear?
2 How many excuses did you hear?

3 How many apologies did you hear?
4 How many offers did you hear?
5 How many explanations did you hear?

Now listen to the dialogue and answer the Impression questions.

When you have answered the first group of questions, listen again and give one example of a complaint, an excuse, an apology, and offer and an explanation.

I   Focus questions

The word 'sorry' has many uses in English. Here are some examples from the Dialogue.

ROGER   I'm afraid I'm not happy with my room.
CLERK   I'm *sorry* about that, sir.
ROGER   Look, I'm *sorry*, but I'd like another room.
CLERK   I'm *sorry*, sir, but I'm afraid 43 is the only single room available at present.

Is the word 'sorry' used in the same way in all three cases? Is the word 'sorry' necessary in all three cases? Now listen to more people using the word 'sorry' and decide whether they are: apologising; expressing sympathy; asking for repetition; expressing sarcasm; getting attention.

J   Discussion

If you were the manager referred to by the clerk in the dialogue, what exactly would you do when you were told about the incident?

Why do you think it was that Mr Hart was given such an unsatisfactory room when he had booked a room three weeks before?

Have you ever stayed in a hotel or boarding house? Have you ever worked in one?

If you were going to London for two weeks, would you prefer to stay in a big hotel or a small hotel? Explain why.

Listening activity 🔊

K   Comprehension

Here are eight statements referring to the interview. Decide whether they are true or false:

1 The hotel was described in the brochure as old-fashioned.
2 The brochure suggests that the staff are very polite.
3 The range of food on the menu was rather limited.
4 Mr and Mrs Wilson experienced communication problems with the staff.
5 All the staff were foreign.
6 Mr and Mrs Wilson got home later than they had expected.
7 Mr Wilson thinks he is wasting his time writing this letter.
8 Mr Wilson does not think that the Isle of Wight is a good place for a holiday.

L   Gap dictation

The manager of Happytours Ltd, has sent for his secretary to discuss a letter of complaint. He has asked her to make notes of complaints that should be investigated. Listen to the letter and complete the notes the secretary should make.

1 We _____ _____ the hotel _____ _____ your brochure _____ _____ _____, medium-sized hotel with a magnificent _____ _____ the sea.

2 In fact, the hotel is situated _____ _____ _____ _____ _____ from the sea.

3 Wine _____ _____, but _____ exorbitant _____.

4 The majority of staff _____ _____, and virtually incapable _____ _____ the English language.

5 In addition to this, we were _____ _____ with the arrangements for _____ _____ _____.

M   Writing activity

Listen to Mr Wilson's letter once more. Can you list his complaints?

N   Practice activity

Here are some facts which are relevant to the complaints mentioned in Mr Wilson's letter:

1 The chef had resigned unexpectedly two days before Mr and Mrs Wilson's arrival at the hotel.
2 There had been certain other difficulties with staff the previous week and the hotel was forced to take on temporary staff.
3 The ferry due to take Mr and Mrs Wilson home was held up owing to an industrial dispute.

Imagine you work for Happytours. Write a polite reply to Mr Wilson't letter, regretting that he was not pleased, explaining why the problems arose and promising better service in the future.

It's not good enough!

Summary

In this unit we practise making complaints.
Imagine you bought a ball-point pen and when you got home, you found it didn't work. You take it back to the shop and the assistant says: 'Can I help you?' What would you say?

In this unit, too, we practise using 'should have' and 'shouldn't have'.

Example:
'Oh, I *should have sent* my aunt a birthday card' – but you didn't.
'Oh dear, I *shouldn't have said* that' – but you did.

Explain when these constructions might be useful.

Note also the verbs 'turn' and 'cut' used as phrasal verbs:
to turn off, to turn on, to turn down, to turn away, to turn out, to cut down, to cut off, to cut out.

Can you think of a situation where we might *turn* somebody *down* and another where we might *cut* something *off*?

UNIT 10 Sales and auctions

Reading activity

THE CHINESE BOWL

1 Mr Fox had spent the last 20 years of his working life as manager of Dougal's, the gentleman's tailor in the High Street. When he retired, he bought a dilapidated farm cottage, with a yard and a small field some five miles out of the town. There he planned to keep a few chickens, grow his own vegetables
5 and pretend he earned his living from agriculture. In fact his pension was index-linked and his income was quite sufficient to provide for the simple life-style that suited his wife, Amelia, and himself.

It was while clearing out the old barn on the far side of the yard that he made an interesting discovery. In a corner, under some old sacks, he found some
10 large fragments of an antique bowl. Intrigued, he took them into the kitchen and, much to the annoyance of his wife, washed the mud off them in the kitchen sink. That evening he spread newspapers over the kitchen table and painstakingly stuck the fragments together. Two pieces were missing, but even Mr Fox's wife, who did not share his enthusiasm for antiques, had to
15 admit that the bowl looked rather splendid.

Two days later, having demolished the barn, Mr Fox was digging over the ground in preparation for the installation of a greenhouse, when he discovered the two missing pieces. When he had stuck them in position the bowl looked so fine that Amelia agreed to its being placed on the sideboard in the sitting-
20 room, in front of the window.

A few days later a stranger, wearing a dark suit, knocked at the door. 'That bowl in the window. You wouldn't be interested in selling it, I suppose?' he asked.
Amelia called her husband.
25 'Selling it?' said Mr Fox. 'No thanks. To tell the truth, I'm rather fond of it.'

However the stranger's interest in the bowl decided Mr Fox on a certain course of action. 'Now, if that chap was interested in buying it, we might have something a bit special here,' he said. 'Have you got any film left in your camera, my love?'

30 Amelia lent her husband her camera and he took several photographs of the bowl, which he sent off to Sotheby's in London. I should explain that Sotheby's is a well-known firm that frequently holds auction sales of antiques and works of art.

A few days later he received a reply. Sotheby's were extremely interested in
35 the bowl and would like to send an expert to inspect it. The expert duly arrived and confirmed that it was indeed something special. It was a Chinese Ming fish bowl, dating back to around 1590 and might be expected to fetch a five-figure sum at auction. The expert gave Mr Fox a receipt and took the bowl back with him to London.

40 A week later two more visitors called, serious-looking men in identical dark blue raincoats, wearing identical dark blue hats.
'Detective Inspector Simpson and Detective Sergeant Thomas,' said the older of the two men. 'Mr Fox? I understand you found this bowl recently.'

He produced one of Mr Fox's photographs.
45 'Yes, that's right. Is anything wrong, Inspector?' Mr Fox looked nervously from one detective to the other. Being questioned by the police was a novel experience.
'The fact is,' the Inspector went on, 'that bowl is stolen property. It disappeared from the Victoria and Albert Museum in 1965.'
50 'Oh, my goodness . . .' stammered Mr Fox.

So the bowl never reached the auction room and Mr Fox never received the five-figure sum that had been mentioned. However, he framed one of the photographs he had taken and placed it on the mantelpiece. And if you visit the Victoria and Albert Museum one day, you will be able to see the bowl itself
55 proudly displayed with other souvenirs of that great Chinese civilisation.

A Questions

1 What sort of things do you imagine Mr Fox sold when he was working?
2 Why was inflation not a great worry to Mr Fox?
3 What do you think the stranger who knocked at Mr Fox's door did for a living?
4 What would you imagine Mr Fox wanted a greenhouse for?
5 Explain what happens at an auction sale.
6 In one respect it might be considered that Mr Fox was unlucky. What often happens when someone recovers stolen property?
7 Give an example of a five-figure sum.

B Vocabulary exercise

1 Mr Fox bought a *dilapidated* cottage. (line 3) Think of some more things that might become dilapidated.
2 At what age do people usually receive a *pension* in your country?
3 Mr Fox found some *fragments* of an old bowl. (line 10) Think of some other things that might break into fragments.
4 Why might the police decide to make a *painstaking* search of a wooded area?
5 Mr Fox told the stranger who knocked at the door that he was *rather fond of* the bowl. (line 25) Think of something you are rather fond of.

6 Would you expect two brothers to have *identical* fingerprints? Give your reasons.

7 What caused Mr Fox to *stammer*. (line 50)

8 Think of some places in your country where tourists or visitors might buy *souvenirs*.

C Vocabulary exercise

Here are ten excerpts from the Reading activity. In the exercise that follows, choose the word or words that could be substituted for the one in italics.

1 When he *retired* he bought a farm cottage. (line 2)
  a went away
  b stopped work
  c withdrew
  d retreated

2 There he planned to *keep* a few chickens. (line 4)
  a have
  b raise
  c bring up
  d grow

3 His income was quite sufficient to provide for the simple life-style that *suited* his wife. (line 6)
  a fitted
  b satisfied
  c appropriated
  d convenienced

4 He found some large fragments of *an antique* bowl. (line 9)
  a an ancient and valuable
  b an elderly and valuable
  c a pre-historic and valuable
  d a very old and valuable

5 He spread newpapers over the table and *stuck* the fragments together. (line 12)
  a joined
  b pushed
  c put
  d fixed

6 Amelia Fox had to admit that the bowl looked *rather* splendid. (line 14)
  a fairly
  b quite
  c a bit
  d completely

7 The bowl looked so fine that Amelia agreed to its being *placed* on the sideboard in the sitting-room (line 18)
  a put
  b situated
  c positioned
  d sited

8 'You wouldn't be interested in selling that bowl, I *suppose*?' (line 22)
  a believe
  b imagine
  c think
  d expect

9 Amelia *lent* her husband her camera. (line 30)
  a gave
  b contributed
  c borrowed
  d offered

10 The expert gave Mr Fox *a receipt*. (line 38)
  a a recipe
  b an acknowledgement
  c a signed statement
  d a prescription

D Discussion

Sotheby's is a firm that specialises in running auction sales of fine-quality antiques and works of art.

Do big shops in your country have 'sales'?
At what time of year do the sales occur?
What sort of things can you buy there?
Have you ever bought anything at a sale?
Was it a successful purchase?

E Practice activity

Look at this sentence:
There he *planned to keep* a few chickens . . . (line 4)

It is sometimes difficult to remember whether certain verbs are followed by the infinitive, the infinitive without 'to', or '-ing'.

This exercise will give you practice in using some of these verbs.

Which of the expressions below (a, b, or c) could be used to complete the sentence?

Sotheby's auction rooms

1 He let me
   a to borrow his bicycle
   b borrow his bicycle
   c borrowing his bicycle

2 She refused
   a coming to Paris
   b come to Paris
   c to come to Paris

3 He suggested
   a to ask you for information
   b asking you for information
   c ask you for information

4 She hesitated
   a to ask for the money
   b asking for the money
   c ask for the money

5 He decided
   a tell the truth
   b telling the truth
   c to tell the truth

6 He admitted
   a stealing the vase
   b to steal the vase
   c steal the vase

7 He delayed
   a paying his bill till the end of the month
   b to pay his bill till the end of the month
   c pay his bill till the end of the month

8 She enjoyed
   a to listen to the music
   b listen to the music
   c listening to the music

9 I expected
   a to see you there
   b seeing you there
   c see you there

10 He made me
   a come to the party
   b to come to the party
   c coming to the party

11 He forced me
   a give him the money
   b giving him the money
   c to give him the money

12 He denied
   a to stab the policeman
   b stabbing the policman
   c stab the policeman

F Practice activity

Now you are going to have the chance to take the part of a witness in a court case.

For many years, in Britain, as in other countries, high-value coins were made of silver or gold. In England the pound sterling (£) was represented by a gold sovereign.

Mr Fox was a keen coin-collector and a prominent member of the local coin club. One evening he was asked to give a talk on the subject of 'British coins from 1700 to the present day'. He took along a number of his coins to illustrate his talk. During the interval, he left his coins unattended in their case on the platform and went into the club canteen. When he returned to the lecture room, he noticed young Mr Silvester examining the coins. As soon as Mr Silvester saw Mr Fox, he started guiltily, blushed and walked away. Subsequently Mr Fox found that two of his gold sovereigns were missing. He was very upset and accused Mr Silvester of stealing them. The case came to court and here is an extract from the trial. Counsel for the defence is cross-examining Mr Fox. You take the part of Mr Fox:

C FOR D   Now, Mr Fox. How long have you known the accused?

MR FOX

C FOR D   Were you on friendly terms with him?

MR FOX

C FOR D   And you came along on the evening in question to give a talk. Am I correct?

MR FOX

C FOR D   And what was the subject of your talk?

MR FOX

C FOR D   And how long did you speak for?

MR FOX

C FOR D   And what happened then?

MR FOX

C FOR D   Did Mr Silvester accompany you into the room where you took your refreshment?

MR FOX

C FOR D   And where was Mr Silvester when you returned to the lecture-room?

MR FOX

C FOR D   What was he doing?

MR FOX

C FOR D   What was his reaction when he saw you?

MR FOX

C FOR D   Why do you think this was?

MR FOX

C FOR D   When exactly did you discover that two of your coins were missing?

MR FOX

C FOR D   Did you see Mr Silvester take the coins?

MR FOX

C FOR D   Of course you didn't, Mr Fox, because Mr Silvester never took the coins. The truth is that during the time the coins were left unattended, *anyone* could have walked up to that platform and helped themselves. Am I correct?

MR FOX

C FOR D   Thank you, Mr Fox.

Do you think Mr Silvester was eventually found guilty of stealing the coins? Give your reasons.

G Practice activity

Ask and answer these questions:

1 Ask why Mr Fox had brought his coins to the club.
2 Answer the question.
3 Ask why Mr Fox had been asked to give a talk.
4 Ask why Mr Fox didn't take his coins into the canteen with him.
5 Ask what Mr Fox was doing when the coins were stolen.
6 Give a possible answer to this question.
7 Ask where Mr Silvester was standing when Mr Fox went back to the lecture-room.
8 Answer the question.
9 Ask why Mr Fox didn't accuse Mr Silvester at once of taking the coins.
10 Answer the question.

H Practice activity

Note these extracts from the Reading activity:

. . . while clearing out the old barn . . . he *made* an interesting discovery.
Sotheby's is a well-known firm that frequently *holds* auction sales of antiques and works of art.

The verbs 'hold' and 'make' are frequently used with prepositions and adverbs. For example:

Lucille took the dress off the rack and *held it up* in front of her. 'That's pretty,' she said.

The Great Train Robbers *held up* the mail train and got away with more than £1 000 000.

The road was uneven and the bus shook and rattled. '*Hold on to* my arm,' said Peter's father.

Jenny was about to lock the door. '*Hold on* a moment,' said Tom. 'I've forgotten my keys.'

Bullets spattered the wall above Thompson's head. 'I'm afraid we won't be able to *hold them off* much longer, Captain,' he muttered.

'We've still got 200 rounds of ammunition,' replied the Captain. 'We must *hold out* till nightfall.'

'*Hold out* your hand,' cried Marti, 'and I'll give you a surprise.'

As soon as Jenkins was well away from the prison, he *made for* the coast.

Sue examined the letter carefully. 'I can't *make out* this signature, I'm afraid,' she said.

'Haagenson's never been in Italy in his life,' said the Inspector. 'He *made up* the story to protect his girl friend.'

'Look, to *make up for* your disappointment, I'll buy you an ice cream.'

Replace the words in italics by suitable expressions with 'hold' or 'make'.

1 Elaine got into the car. '*Wait* a moment,' said Stan, 'I must check the oil.'
2 Shots rained in on the Brazilian goal from all angles, but somehow the defence *remained unbeaten.*
3 The car stopped and the driver rolled down the window. 'Where are you *going to*?' he asked the hitch-hiker.
4 'When was Shakespeare born?' asked the teacher. John *raised* his hand and the teacher nodded in his direction.
   '1564,' said John. The teacher smiled. 'Good,' he said.
5 'Why did he buy you the fur coat?' asked Lucinda.
   'To *compensate for* not taking me to the Bahamas,' said Deborah.
6 'What's happened, sir?' cried Jenkins. 'You're as white as a sheet.'
   'The security van.' said Sir Arthur, 'They *robbed* the security van and they've got the gold.'
7 'Excuse me, waiter,' said George, 'I can't *read* this item on the bill.'
8 That's not his real name. He *invented it*.

Dialogue 🔘

George and Enid have just bumped into each other as they were struggling to get off a number 12 London bus. Listen to their conversation and then answer these Impression questions.

Mandolin

Guitar

Sales and auctions

I Impression questions

1 Are George and Enid old friends?
2 Have they met recently?
3 Why did Enid think George had bought a guitar?
4 Do you think George and Enid share the same interests?
5 Enid interrupted George several times. What do you think he was going to say in these excerpts?

    a GEORGE Not a guitar, Enid. A mandolin. Quite old. No strings at the moment . . . but I can easily _____ .

    b ENID I want a pair of those very pointed shoes they used to wear in the fifties.

    GEORGE Sorry, Enid, I'm afraid I don't _____ .

J Focus questions

Enid thought that a mandolin must be a musical instrument, because it had strings and was played. In these conversations, there are similar clues. Look for the clues when you answer the Focus questions.

1 PHILLIP What is that ugly-looking thing?
  ALEX It's a rutabaga.
  PHILLIP What on earth are you going to do with it?
  ALEX Peel it and cook it, of course.

  Question: *What is a rutabaga?*

2 ALEX What a big parcel! Have you bought a do-it-yourself kit?
  PHILLIP No, it's only a plane.
  ALEX What are you going to do with it?
  PHILLIP Get rid of all the rough edges on the old bench I've just bought.

  Question *What is a plane?*

3 PHILLIP I've never seen that before. What is it?
  ALEX Moisturiser.
  PHILLIP Where are you going to put it? On the plants?
  ALEX No, Phillip. On my face.

  Question: *What is moisturiser?*

4 ALEX I'm glad you remembered to buy a lead, Phillip. It's just what we need.
  PHILLIP It's just the right length, isn't it? Now we can train the puppy.
  ALEX Right. You can take him for a long walk in the morning.

  Question: *What is a lead?*

5 PHILLIP This flat is always cold.
  ALEX We have too many windows and no double glazing. Our neighbours have double glazing and their house is always warm.
  PHILLIP I like fresh air, but not cold air. Do you know anyone we could consult about double glazing?

  Question: *What is double glazing?*

K Discussion

The pointed shoes that Enid refers to are an interesting example of a fashion that came and went. They say fashion goes round in a circle, so perhaps the pointed shoes will come back one day.

Think of some other fashions that came and went, especially the sort of clothes young people might go to look for in a market where second-hand clothes can be bought.

Are you particularly attracted by any of the styles that used to be fashionable, but aren't now?

What is there about the different styles in the photographs that would make them particularly suitable or unsuitable for life today?

Listening activity 📼

L   Comprehension

Here are eight statements referring to the dialogue. Decide whether they are true or false.

1   There will probably be more customers than usual in Franklin's on Tuesday.
2   You can buy a wide range of goods at Franklin's.
3   You can get a Moulinex mixer for only £8.
4   An electric kettle will cost you £40.
5   You can buy bedclothes at Franklin's.
6   You can buy porcelain tea-sets for £21.15.
7   You can buy six wine glasses for £2.45.
8   Knives and forks are being sold in the sale.

M   Gap dictation

Listen to this advertisement for Franklin's famous summer sale. Fill in the very important missing information.

We've got fantastic bargains for all the family and for every room in your cosy little home.
Let's start with your kitchen. Genuine well-known mixers (1)_____ _____ toasters (2)_____
_____ _____; electric kettles (3)_____ _____. Or what about a fantastic pressure-cooker
(4)_____ _____.

And your bedroom. A super selection of bedspreads (5)_____ _____.
Pure woollen blankets (6)_____ _____, a fabulous selection of sheets in pairs (7)_____

_____, and genuine feather pillows (8)_____
_____ _____.

Don't forget your dining-room. (9)_____ _____
English-bone china tea-sets (10)_____ _____; six super quality wine-glasses . . . (11)_____; _____
_____ stainless-steel cutlery sets for (12)_____
_____

You can't afford to miss this sale.

N   Writing activity

Listen to the advertisement again. Make a short list of the goods offered for sale.

O   Writing activity

A character in a story by Somerset Maugham says: 'The money you spend on necessities is boring. The money that is amusing to spend is the money you spend on luxuries.'

What do you consider to be necessities?
What do you consider to be luxuries?
Of the necessities you have to buy, which are the most boring?
Of the luxuries you sometimes buy, which do you enjoy most? Why?
When would you do without necessities to buy luxuries?
When would you do without luxuries to buy necessities?
Do you enjoy going shopping?
Do you prefer shopping in supermarkets or big stores, or in small shops and boutiques?

Write about 250 words on 'Shopping'.

Sales and auctions UNIT 10

Summary

In this unit we establish whether certain common verbs are followed by the infinitive, the infinitive without 'to', or '-ing'.

Here is the list of these verbs:

He *let me have* the money.
She *made him return* the book.

She *suggested (my) coming* to see you.
He *denied taking* the stamps.
He *delayed making* a decision as long as possible.
She *enjoyed going* to parties.
He *admitted making* a mistake.

She *hesitated to mention* it at the time.
I *decided to see* the doctor about it.
He *refused to discuss* the matter.
He *expects to see* you at the meeting.
They *forced her to give* them the information they wanted.

Look at this sentence: 'He forced her to hand over the papers.' Which of the verbs above might be used to express the same idea?

We also practise using past tenses, particularly the past continuous. This is a difficult tense to learn to use effectively. Remember that it is normally used in combination with the simple past.

Examples:
Mr Silvester *was looking* at the coins when I came into the room.

What *were you doing* at the hospital when I saw you there yesterday?

Study this diagram:

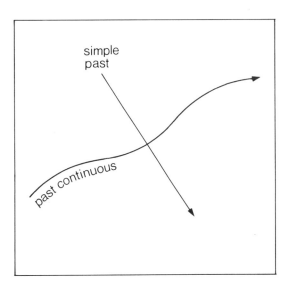

It is intended to illustrate the relationship between the past continuous and the simple past. Explain that relationship.

Note also these useful phrasal verbs with 'hold' and 'make':
to hold up, to hold on (to), to hold off, to make up for.

Give an example of something we might *make up* and something we might have difficulty in *making out.*

UNIT 11 Talking to people

Don't sit in an empty seat – sit beside somebody

Reading activity

STARTING A CONVERSATION

1 Johannes had come to England to improve his English. He had studied the language for five years in his own country and he could understand a written text quite well. What he needed above all was practice in conversation.

He enrolled at a school for foreign students and the school found him a home
5 with an English family. The family were pleasant and friendly and he was delighted to discover that there was a pretty daughter, only a year or so younger than himself. That first night, as he lay in bed, he was filled with optimism.

A few days later, however, when his class teacher, Mr Price, asked him how he
10 was getting on, he had to confess that he felt a little disappointed. 'By Sunday,' said Johannes, 'I'll have been here for two weeks, but I've had very little conversation practice.'
'Aren't you living with an English family?' asked Mr Price.
'Yes, I am,' replied Johannes, 'but they're always busy.'
15 'Aren't there any young people in the family?'
'Yes, there's a daughter of 17, but she leaves home at eight o'clock in the morning and she spends every evening with her friends.'

'Well,' said Mr Price, 'you'll just have to learn to get into conversation with strangers.'

20 'But how?' asked Johannes, 'and where?'

'You travel on buses, don't you?' suggested Mr Price.

'Yes,' said Johannes doubtfully.

'Don't sit in an empty seat, sit beside somebody. You can often have marvellous conversations on buses.'

25 'It's difficult to know what to talk about,' said Johannes. 'That *is* a problem,' agreed Mr Price. 'You can always start with the weather, but that won't keep you going for long. You've got to read the papers, watch television, find out what English people are talking about. Then after you've talked about the weather, you can ask a question.'

30 'How do you mean?' Johannes looked puzzled.

'Well, let's imagine you read a story in the paper about a murder case or a political election. You could say: "I wonder if they'll find Barrett guilty?" or "Do you think Jordan will win?" – something like that. People like being asked their opinion about things. Or you can try talking about a programme

35 you saw on television. "Did you see that play on television last night? Good, wasn't it?" English people won't usually start a conversation, but often they're quite happy to chat, provided *you* start talking to them.'

Johannes nodded 'I see what you mean,' he said thoughtfully.

'One more thing,' Mr Price continued, 'older people are nearly always easier

40 to get into conversation with than younger ones. The young are terribly wrapped up in their own lives. But the older ones can't resist talking about the good old days. When they were young, the sun was always shining, everybody was always good-humoured. There wasn't so much money, but everyone enjoyed themselves. Perhaps it's the same in your country?'

45 Johannes smiled. 'I think old people are the same all over the word,' he said.

A Questions

1 Could Johannes speak English well?

2 Can you explain why Johannes was feeling a bit disappointed?

3 So what did Mr Price suggest?

4 What steps did Mr Price advise Johannes to take in order to find suitable topics of conversation?

5 What method does Mr Price suggest for actually *starting* the conversation?

6 What does Mr Price mean when he says: 'The young are terribly wrapped up in their own lives.'? (line 40)

7 Do you think Mr Price is correct?

8 Do you think the advice Mr Price gives Johannes would be equally suitable for a girl? Give your reasons.

B Vocabulary exercise

1 Johannes *enrolled* at school for foreign students. Have you ever enrolled for any courses? What were they?

2 He was filled with *optimism*. He felt optimistic. What are you feeling optimitic about at the moment? What is the opposite of optimistic?

3 'Yes,' said Johannes *doubtfully*. We might say: 'I'm doubtful if it will happen.' What might we be talking about?

4 Johannes looked *puzzled*. We are often puzzled because we don't know how something works or why something happened. Think of a situation when you might be puzzled.

5 In court, the accused is found '*guilty*' or '*not guilty*'. Think of a current court case in your country. Do you think the accused will be found 'guilty' or 'not guilty'?

6 To *chat* is to have a pleasant conversation. Who have you had a chat with recently? What did you talk about?

7 We can *wrap up* a parcel. What was the last parcel you wrapped up?. Who was it for and what was in it?

C   Vocabulary exercise

Here are seven excerpts from the Reading activity. You should study them carefully, looking at the meaning of the words as they are used. Then find the *two* answers that *cannot* replace the word or words in italics.

1 What he needed *above all* was practice in conversation. (line 3)
   a over all
   b particularly
   c especially
   d after all

2 You can always start with the weather but that won't keep you *going* for long. (line 26)
   a running
   b talking
   c moving
   d chatting

3 'How do you mean?' Johannes looked *puzzled*. (line 30)
   a worried
   b strange
   c uncertain
   d unsure

4 . . . but often they're *quite happy to chat*. (line 36)
   a ready to talk
   b prepared to have a conversation
   c amused at the thought of talking
   d pleased to listen

5 Johannes *nodded*. (line 38)
   a accepted
   b agreed
   c acknowledged
   d understood

6 The older ones can't *resist* talking about the good old days. (line 41)
   a keep themselves from
   b help themselves to
   c stop themselves
   d ask themselves to

7 . . . everybody was always *good-humoured*. (line 42)
   a cheerful
   b laughing
   c humorous
   d in a good mood

D   Discussion

Many people would find it difficult to start a conversation with total strangers, even in their own language. But it is only natural that foreign visitors to this country should ask questions, and in England people are usually very helpful.

Casual conversation is something that occurs when two or more people are interested in the same subject. Can you think of some interesting subjects in the news at the present time?

Practise starting a conversation about two or three of these subjects as the writer suggests.

Why do you think old people spend so much time talking about the good old days? Do you think life was really so much better then?

E   Practice activity

Johannes says: 'By Sunday *I'll have been* here for two weeks.'

Look at the situations below and make more sentences like the one above:

1 Tim is on holiday in Switzerland. It is Tuesday morning. Tim still has 1000 francs, but he is spending 200 francs a day. By when will he have spent all his money?

2 Judy is getting married. It's going to be a big wedding and 160 guests are expected. Judy is writing 40 invitations every evening. By when will she have sent out all the invitations if she starts on Monday?

3 On Saturday morning Tom's wife went away for a few days. The only thing Tom can cook is eggs. There are 40 eggs in the refrigerator and Tom is eating eight eggs a day. By when will he have finished the eggs in the refrigerator?

4 It's 10.00 a.m. Dolly has a 30-page report to type and she can manage 10 pages in an hour. By when will she have finished typing the report?

5 Natalie is reading an interesting murder story. Gwen wants to read it too, but Natalie is only at page 70. The book has 190 pages and Natalie can read 40 pages a day. It is Sunday morning. By when will Natalie have finished the book?

6 It is November and Dr Barnes has 24 patients in his surgery waiting to see him. He spends 10 minutes with each patient. Surgery starts at 6.00 p.m. By when will he have seen all his patients?

7 Mr Chandler is a tailor. He's making a suit for Mr Andrews. It takes Mr Chandler a week to make a suit. Mr Andrews chose the cloth first thing on Monday morning. When will Mr Chandler have finished the suit?
(*Note:* in this case, 'a week' equals five working days.)

8 Sonia is taking an examination. She must answer six questions and she has $2\frac{1}{2}$ hours. She finds that she needs half an hour for each question. Will she have answered all the questions by the time the exam finishes? If not, how many questions will she have left unanswered?

F   Practice activity

Mr Price says: '*Aren't* you living with an English family?' and his next question is: '*Aren't* there any young people in the family?'

We often use the negative form to indicate surprise when we are asking questions. Practise asking more questions beginning with 'Aren't . . . ?'

1 There is a party on Saturday evening, but someone told you that Sonia isn't coming. What question do you ask Sonia when you see her?

2 You intended to get a ticket for the concert but you heard someone say that all the tickets had been sold. What do you say?

3 Tom was going to buy Peter's car. Someone said that Tom had changed his mind at the last minute and that Peter was cross about it. What do you say when you see Tom?

4 Freda and her husband were going to San Francisco for their holiday. You hear that they have changed their plans. What do you say when you see Freda?

5 You are having a meal in a restaurant. You notice some rather beautiful strawberries and you fancy some. But then the strawberries disappear, another customer asks for strawberries and you see the waiter shrug his shoulders. What do you say to the waiter?

6 You have a friend called Peter and another friend called Eva. Eva is flying from New York to London on Saturday. Peter had agreed to meet her. Someone tells you he's changed his mind. What do you say to Peter?

7 You have just joined a new class to study for an examination in English. You thought there would be one or two Italians in the class. It seems you were wrong. What do you say?

8 You are at a big railway station in London. It is 11.45 p.m. and you want to catch a train to Dulwich, but there are no more trains listed on the indicator board. You see a ticket collector. What is the question you ask him?

G   Practice activity

The verb 'run' is frequently used with prepositions and adverbs. For example:

I'm sorry, we've *run out of* milk, so you'll have to have your coffee black.

'Whatever happened to Henry's car?'
'Unfortunately, he *ran into* the back of a post office van.'

A tall, thin youth grabbed Tom's briefcase and *ran off* with it. Tom *ran after* him, but he lost him in the crowd.

'Don't you like Theodore?'
'I can't stand the man. He's always *running down* the firm he works for.'

'Did you get the diamonds?'
'I'm afraid not. We *ran up against* some unexpected problems.'

'Don't mention her cat – it was *run over* last week.'

Mr Potter wore old-fashioned spectacles. The local children used to stand outside his shop and shout 'Four eyes, four eyes,' until he came out. Then they *ran away*.

Poor old Bob was *run in* for speeding last week.

Replace the words in italics by suitable expressions with 'run'. Use each expression once only:

1   'Why did you hit Cyril?'
    'He was *criticising you,* Mildred.'
2   'Are you going to bake a cake?'
    'I can't. We've *got no flour left.*'
3   If those children aren't careful, one of them is going to be *knocked down* by a car.
4   'What happened to the new bus stop?'
    'A bus *hit* it.'
5   I'm afraid we can't go ahead with building the new extension yet. We've *encountered* difficulties over getting planning permission.
6   As soon as the two young men saw the policeman, they *sprinted* in the direction of the river. The policeman *chased* them.
7   I was once *prosecuted* for riding my bicycle at night without lights.

Dialogue 🔊

Anne shares a London flat with three other girls. She has just returned from work. Listen to her conversation.

H   Impression questions

1   What do you think was happening at the flat when Anne got home?
2   Do you think Anne was surprised?
3   How do you think her friend Jean was feeling?
4   What is the difference between 'asking a few friends over' and 'having a party'?
5   Who do you think Mary and Helen are?
6   Jean said, 'You know what happens.' What do you think she meant?
7   Was Anne interested in seeing her friends?
8   Why was Anne looking for a quiet place?
9   What kind of job do you think Anne has?
10 What kind of job do you think Jean has?

I   Focus questions

Listen again to Anne's conversation and notice the words that are stressed. Underline them.

JEAN   Isn't this fun, Anne?
ANNE   Isn't what fun?
JEAN   The party, of course.
ANNE   Nobody told me about a party.

Now look at these short dialogues and underline the words in Anne's speeches that should be stressed. After you have checked with your teacher, practise saying the dialogues with a partner.

1   JEAN   I asked you to do the washing-up.
    ANNE   Yes, but you didn't tell me to do it, did you?
2   JEAN   Why didn't you come to our party?
    ANNE   Because you didn't ask me.
3   JEAN   Didn't Helen ask you to the party?
    ANNE   No, nobody asked me.
4   JEAN   A lot of my friends were there.
    ANNE   What about mine?
5   JEAN   Some of my friends arrived quite early.
    ANNE   I'm sure most of mine arrived late.

J   Discussion

Compare your own language with English. Do you use stress in a similar way to indicate your feelings?

This short dialogue demonstrates how easy it is in English to change the meaning and tone of what you are saying by altering the stress.

Take another short English sentence:
'I don't want to go to the zoo.'
Try saying the sentence with stress on different words. Decide what possible variations there are and how they would alter the meaning.

Talking to people

Listening activity 🔾

K Comprehension

Here are eight statements referring to the
conversation. Decide whether they are true or false.

1 Listeners can hear Mr Humphries talking on
   the radio.
2 Mr Humphries has been to Spain more than
   once.
3 Mr Humphries has been learning Spanish for
   several years.
4 Mr Humphries is fluent in Spanish.
5 The BBC publishes books.
6 The Professor believes that it would be easy for
   Mr Humphries to have conversations with
   Spanish people if he lived in Spain.
7 The Professor advises Mr Humphries to check
   his Spanish pronunciation by using a cassette
   recorder.
8 The Professor advises Mr Humphries to find
   some Spanish speakers in London and practise
   talking to them.

L Gap dictation

Listen again to this part of Professor Watson's
phone-in programme and write the missing parts.

PROFESSOR
WATSON   I always think that (1)_____
_____ _____ is (2)_____ _____
_____ _____ _____. Now, you
(3)_____ _____ _____
_____ _____ _____ by sitting in a
classroom (4)_____ _____ _____.
I think
(5)_____ _____ _____ _____ -
_____ _____ _____ _____ _ -
_____ using the language.

ALBERT
HUMPHRIES   That's all (6)_____ _____ if you
live in the (7)_____ where they speak
the language, but (8)_____ _____.

PROFESSOR
WATSON   Yes, I understand the problem.
(9)_____ _____ _____ _____
_____ _____ _____ _____

where the language is spoken, you
have to reach a certain standard.

M Writing activity

Listen to the conversation again. Then write a short
summary of the advice that the Professor gives to
Mr Humphries on improving his command of the
Spanish language.

N Writing activity

Here are some different ways of studying a
language:

1 Buy a book.
   Problems: Pronunciation may be a difficulty.
                  Requires great self-discipline.

2 Buy a course on records or on tape.
   Problem: Could be expensive.

3 Go to an evening class.
   Problem: By the time the next lesson comes
                round, you tend to forget what you
                learnt last time.

4 Go to the country where the language is
   spoken.
   Problem: A bit expensive and time-
                consuming. Also it might be
                diffficult to find a nice family to live
                with.

5 Go to a school in the country where the
   language is spoken.
   Problem: Expensive and time-consuming.

Now imagine that an English friend of yours very
much wants to learn *your* language. Write him/her a
letter 150–250 words long, advising him/her the
best way to do it.

Summary

In this unit we practise using the future in the past. The future in the past is always used together with a time expression.

Examples:

The doctor *will have seen* all his patients *by 6.00 p.m.*

By the weekend I *will have finished* reading the book. Then I'll give it to you.

In another two years Tom *will have left* school, and I hope *he'll have found* a job.

Can you explain when we use this tense?

We also practise asking questions beginning with 'Aren't . . . ?'
Example: 'Aren't you coming with us to the park?'
Can you explain the difference between this question and:
'Are you coming with us to the park?'

Note also some useful phrasal verbs with 'run':
run out of, run into, run off, run after, run down, run up against, run over, run away, run in.

Can you think of a situation in which you might be run over?
What might a housewife run out of?

UNIT 12 Taking chances

Reading activity

GAMBLING FEVER

1   The tourists pause and watch, wide-eyed, as the smart lady and gentleman
emerge from the dark limousine, walk up the steps and disappear through the
impressive entrance to the Casino at Monte Carlo. Inside, beneath the elegant
chandeliers, the roulette wheel turns, and crisp new cards are expertly
5   shuffled and dealt. Large sums are often lost and fortunes are occasionally
won.

   In Britain too there are those who have been bitten by the gambling bug.
There *are* casinos, but if you visited one, you would find that many of the
clients were foreign. Perhaps to the Britisher a horse, a dog, or a football team
10 seems more predictable than little balls whizzing round, or cards stacked on
green baize.

   Every Saturday, enormous sums are wagered on the football pools. The mere
collection of the coupons is a massive business operation, and there is a
moment of hush in millions of families around five o'clock when the football
15 results are shown on the television screen. Of course, the vast majority of
punters lose week after week, but they keep on trying hopefully for one big
win.

Then there are the horses. Every day, or almost every day, except Sunday, there is horse-racing in Britain. There are famous meetings, such as the Derby
20 or Royal Ascot in the summer and the Grand National in early spring, attended by huge crowds, and there are comparatively unimportant meetings at small tracks like Newton Abbot, Plumpton or Pontefract. But betting shops throughout the land ensure that it is as easy for a Scotsman in Glasgow or an Englishman in Birmingham to have a bet at one of these small tracks as it is for
25 spectators attending the meeting.

And there are the greyhounds – long, lean, hungry-looking beasts that chase a ridiculous stuffed object, known as a 'hare', round a miniature race track. On a Saturday night, the fashionable stadiums attract several thousand spectators. But somewhere, nearly every day, the dogs are running at almost deserted
30 tracks and the punters are backing their fancies in the betting shops.

Bingo is popular too. Many cinemas have now been converted into bingo halls. You buy a card, numbers are shouted out and the and the winner is the one whose card is completed first.

Of course, there are those who are highly critical of all this gambling, but I
35 must confess that I have a soft spot for the gambler. He has to be something of a philosopher, for he is likely to lose more often than he wins. However, when he does win, he knows a special sort of happiness that has little to do with the amount of money involved. And I sometimes wonder if those who criticise the gambler realise that life itself is an incredible gamble – the biggest gamble of
40 all.

Taking chances

A Questions

1 What do people do at the Casino at Monte Carlo?
2 What would you discover if you paid a visit to a British casino?
3 Why does everybody stop talking for a few minutes on a Saturday afternoon in many British homes?
4 What is the Derby?
5 Why do you think a hare is necessary at greyhound tracks?
6 Why must the gambler be a bit of a philosopher?

B Vocabulary exercise

1 The ladies and gentlemen *emerge* from dark limousines. Can you think when the word 'emerge' might be used when talking about a train?
2 *Crisp* new cards are dealt . . . The word 'crisp' is sometimes used in advertisements for food. For what sort of products?
3 *The vast majority* of punters lose every week. Name some more groups of people who might be referred to as 'the vast majority'.
4 What do people *back* in England?
5 How does the Post Office *ensure* that members of the public pay the postage fee on letters they post?
6 The greyhounds *chase* the hare. Have you ever seen a 'chase' in an old film? What sort of a chase was it? Why might a policeman chase somebody?
7 The writer has a *soft spot* for the gambler. What do you have a soft spot for?

C Vocabulary exercise

Here are seven excerpts from the Reading activity. They are followed by a choice of answers. Read the instructions for each exercise very carefully. They are not all the same.

1 If you visited a casino, you would realise that many of the clients were foreign. (line 8) Which of the following can have *clients?*
   a football clubs
   b lawyers
   c shop-keepers
   d film stars

2 A Scotsman in Glasgow can back a horse at a small race in the south of England. Which of these could you *back?*
   a a friend
   b a politician
   c an enemy
   d a bet

3 But betting shops throughout the land . . . (line 22) Which of these words could replace *throughout?*
   a across
   b including
   c down
   d up

4 But somewhere, almost every day, the dogs are running and the punters are backing their fancies. (line 29) Which of these words could replace *fancies?*
   a impressions
   b choices
   c preferences
   d desires

5 It is as easy for a Scotsman in Glasgow to have a bet . . . (line 23) Which of these words could replace *have?*
   a make
   b do
   c place
   d take

6 Smart ladies and gentlemen emerge from dark limousines. (line 1) Which of these words could replace *smart?*
   a clever
   b fashionable
   c clean
   d well-dressed

7 On a Saturday night, the fashionable stadiums attract several thousand spectators. (line 27) At which of these entertainments could you find *spectators?*
   a a play
   b a football match
   c a swimming competition
   d a film

87

D Discussion

'Life itself is an incredible gamble – the biggest gamble of all.' (line 39)

A punter can choose whether to gamble on a horse or a dog, but in 'the gamble of life' we often have no choice.

Make a list of the things which happen to us in life which are a gamble, but over which we have no control and those moments in life when we *do* have a choice, but are forced to take a gamble.

When you have your list, put the items in order of importance.

E Practice activity

If we had a friend who was determined to gamble, and we thought he was being foolish, we could say: 'Surely you don't think you're going to *win!*'

If we visit a friend and see a shiny new car outside the house which we think *might* be his or hers we could say:
'Surely that's not *your* car outside!'

Here are some more situations. Make similar comments beginning with 'Surely . . . !' (There will be more than one possible answer.)

1 John gave a very unconvincing excuse for not coming to your friend's birthday party. Your friend seems to believe his story . . .

2 You are with Helen and you see Louise. Louise is wearing a new, very expensive-looking fur coat. You find it difficult to believe that she bought it herself . . .

3 You and Helen go to visit Elizabeth for the first time after she got married and moved into her new home. She said the address was 14, Sunny Way, but when you arrive outside the house it looks unoccupied and has two broken windows . . .

4 You arrange to go out with John. You call for him and he says: 'Right, ready then?' But he is wearing very old, dirty clothes and you can't believe he intends to go out without changing . . .

5 Helen has been on a diet. You go with her to an Indian restaurant. She piles the food on her plate and you find it difficult to believe she's going to eat it all . . .

6 Rolf is a fellow student of yours. He is very lazy and didn't work at all hard. The exam results have just come out and you and Helen see him looking very happy . . .

7 You know Kate got married recently. You and Helen see her with a man at least 20 years older than herself. You find it difficult to believe it's her new husband . . .

8 Rail fares went up two months ago and you hear on the radio that the Minister for Transport has made a speech in which he says that the railways are still losing money . . .

F Practice activity

Study this sentence:
The tourists pause and watch, wide-eyed, as the smart lady and gentleman emerge from the limousine, walk up the steps and disappear . . .

Sports commentators, political reporters and advertising men and women often use the simple present tense like this to create a dramatic effect.

Imagine that you are a radio commentator at the Olympic Games and an athlete from your country has just won a gold medal. Describe the presentation ceremony for English-speaking listeners. Begin your commentary like this:
. . . and now we wait for the presentation of the medals for the . . .

G Practice activity

Note these extracts from the text:
. . . the vast majority of punters lose week after week, but they *keep on trying* hopefully for one big win. (line 15)
. . . somewhere almost every day the dogs are running and the punters *are backing* their fancies in the betting shops. (line 29)
The verbs 'keep' and 'back' are frequently used with prepositions and adverbs. For example:

The notice said quite clearly '*Keep off* the grass,' but most people ignored it.

As the young couple came down the steps of the Registry Office, the crowd surged forward. '*Keep back,* please,' said the policeman.

In the first round of the golf tournament, Niklaus scored 75. But he followed this with a 69. You can't *keep* a good professional *down.*

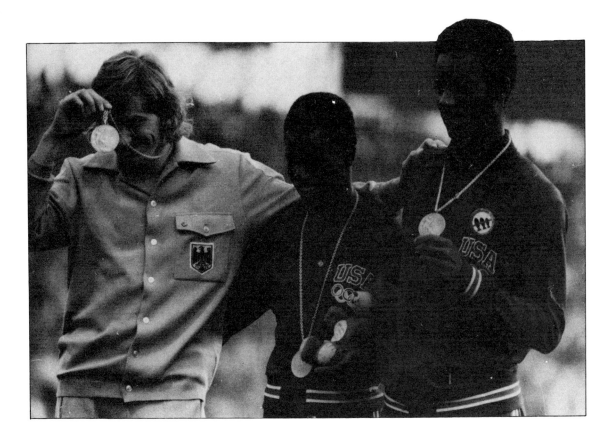

Two men *kept on* interrupting the chairman's speech, so eventually they were asked to leave.

The boys wanted a dog very much. They *kept on at* their father till he bought them one.

She's very tired. The baby *kept* her *up* for several hours last night.

'*Keep out*. Private land,' said the notice. 'What are we going to do now?' asked Pete.

You agreed to buy the car. You can't *back out of* the deal now.

Tell Mr Henderson you think you're worth another £10 a week. I'll *back you up*.

Replace the words in italics by suitable expressions with 'keep' or 'back'. Use each expression once only.

1 The newspaper reporters *continued to pester* the poor woman until she burst into tears.
2 There was a sign on the door which said '*No admittance*'.
3 Let's ask for next Friday off. You speak to the boss. I'll *support you.*
4 When the ambulance arrived at the scene of the accident, a crowd had gathered round the victim. '*Make room, please,*' said the ambulance-man.
5 Jordan signed a written contract and he's not going to *withdraw from* it now.
6 I'm sorry I *delayed your going to bed* for such a long time last night, but I found our discussion very useful.

Dialogue 📼

Kevin and Christine Clark have been married for two years. They are living in a rented flat and are trying to save up the deposit for a flat of their own. Christine is in the kitchen, wondering whether to turn down the oven or not. Listen to their conversation.

H Impression questions

Try to answer as many of the questions as you can. You will be given an opportunity to listen again if you like.

1 Why do you think Kevin was late?
2 How do you think Christine was feeling when Kevin arrived?
3 What was Christine's attitude when she saw the money?
4 Do you think Kevin gave a good reason for gambling?
5 What do you think of Christine's reasons for disliking gambling?
6 Was Kevin really listening to what Christine was saying?
7 Why do you think Kevin's dinner was probably burnt?
8 Do you think Kevin will stop going to the betting shop?
9 Think of two adjectives to describe Christine.
10 Think of two adjectives to describe Kevin.

I Focus questions

In the dialogue, there are many examples of informal and idiomatic English. Here are a few of them:

Where on earth did you get it?
As a matter of fact I did.
How else are we going to save any money?
Surely you aren't serious?
Only too well!
We've been over this again and again.
Come on. Cheer up.

Choose one of these expressions to complete the short dialogues.

1 KEVIN   I sold the car this morning.
   CHRISTINE
   KEVIN   Of course I am. Walking is good for us.

2 CHRISTINE I hope you made a profit.
   KEVIN
   CHRISTINE Would you mind telling me how much?

3 CHRISTINE I don't really understand why you had to sell it.
   KEVIN
   CHRISTINE Do you really think selling the car will help?

4 KEVIN   Don't you realise how expensive everything is now?
   CHRISTINE
   KEVIN   Then why don't you cut down on expenses?

5 CHRISTINE There's no point in discussing anything tonight. I think I'll go to bed.
   KEVIN
   CHRISTINE How can I? Goodnight!

Listening activity 🔘

J Comprehension

Here are eight statements referring to Dr McPherson's evidence. Decide whether they are true or false.

1   Dr McPherson thinks the Government should have looked into the question of gambling at an earlier date.
2   Dr McPherson thinks that people in Glasgow drink too much tea and coffee.
3   There is a shortage of work in Glasgow at the present time.
4   Some of the men are unemployed because they drink too much.
5   Family allowance is supposed to be spent on the children.
6   Dr McPherson sometimes goes to see the families of unemployed workers.
7   Dr McPherson feels that the Government is wrong to allow unemployment benefit to be paid on a Friday.
8   Dr McPherson thinks that horse-racing should be allowed at least once a week.

K Gap dictation

Listen again to the evidence Dr McPherson gave on his investigations into gambling in Britain. Complete his statements.

I (1)_____ _____ _____ put on record my appreciation of the fact that Her Majesty's Government (2)_____ _____ _____ seen fit to set up an enquiry into what I believe to be one of the two great social evils of our time. Working as I do (3)_____ _____ _____ _____ in the great city of Glasgow, I am (4)_____ brought face to face with the consequences of those two great evils: drink and gambling. (5)_____ _____, at the present time, considerable numbers of unemployed persons in the city of Glasgow, (6)_____ _____. Among the (7)_____ there are, naturally, (8)_____ _____ respectable, hard-working men, (9)_____ _____ _____.

L Writing activity

Dr McPherson is very critical of the Government's lack of action regarding the gambling laws.

Taking your facts from Dr McPherson's statement, summarise the problems likely to face a Glasgow family with an unemployed father.

M Writing activity

Write 250–350 words on 'Gambling'.
Here is a suggested plan:
Say what you think about gambling generally.
Explain why people gamble, in your opinion.
Write a paragraph about the awful consequences that can occur.
Say what part gambling plays in your own life.

Summary

In this unit we practise expressing surprise by using 'surely' followed by the negative.

Example:
Surely that's not Peter's car!
Surely you aren't going to eat that banana!

Explain what the situation might be in which each of these remarks was made. Why is the speaker surprised?

We also practise using the simple present for dramatic effect.

Example:
. . . the two young policemen step forward and the President pins the medals on their chests . . .

What is the ceremony? What do you think the two young policemen might have done?

Note also these useful phrasal verbs with 'keep' and 'back':
keep on, keep on at, keep off, keep back, keep down, keep up, keep out, back up, back out of.

Think of something a businessman might want to back out of.
Why might a farmer put up a notice saying 'Keep out'?

Reading activity

Sex Discrimination

The difference can no longer make a difference

1   The Sex Discrimination Act became law on December 29. Generally, employers, educational establishments and those that provide goods, facilities and services to the public e.g. banks, building societies, finance houses and landlords will be breaking the law if they do not provide men and women with
5   the same opportunities and services.

Equality in Employment
Any employer who discriminates on grounds of sex in recruitment, treatment or promotion, will be breaking the law. Employment agencies will not usually be able to label jobs 'for men' or 'for women'.

10   There are only a few exceptions. These include employment in private households, employers with not more than five staff, jobs such as acting and modelling, and situations that need to be confined to one sex for reasons of decency or privacy. Also illegal, in the field of employment, is discrimination on grounds of marriage.

15   ### Equality in Education
Schools, colleges and universities must not discriminate in the facilities they provide. For example, classes in mechanical drawing and home economics must be open to both girls and boys. From September 1st 1976, co-educational schools must not discriminate in their admissions. *It's*
20   *particularly important that parents are aware of their children's rights.*

Equality in Housing, Goods and Services
Generally, those who provide housing, goods, facilities or services to the public will not be allowed to discriminate against customers because of their sex. This applies whether accommodation is being bought or rented and
25   includes hotels, public houses and restaurants.

Equality in Finance
Banks, building societies and finance houses must not treat one sex less favourably than the other in the terms in which credit, mortgages and loans are offered.

30 **Equality in Advertising**
Advertisements may not indicate an intent to discriminate. A job
advertisement using terms such as 'waiter', 'salesgirl', 'postman' or
'stewardess' should make it clear that both men and women are eligible.

The Equal Opportunities Commission
35 The Equal Opportunities Commission will oversee the working of the Sex
Discrimination Act and Equal Pay Act and seek to eliminate discrimination.
Above all, the Commission will help you to know your rights and how to
exercise them.
The Commission's address is:

40 **Equal Opportunities Commission,**
Overseas House,
Quay Street,
Manchester M3 3HN.
Telephone: 061-833 9244.

45 **What you should do now**
Get from Crown Post Offices a free copy of 'A Short Guide to the Sex
Discrimination Act 1973' or fill in the coupon to obtain the free literature that
explains how the Sex Discrimination Act affects you.

The Sex Discrimination Act applies to you! Think
50 ### about it.

A   Questions

1 Is the Sex Discrimination Act now in force?
2 Does the new act apply to a firm employing
four staff?
3 Can an employer refuse to give a woman a job
because she is married?
4 How does the new act affect schools attended
by girls and boys?
5 Do you think the new act might make it easier
for women to borrow money? Give your
reasons.
6 Explain why it is now unacceptable to use
words like waiter or salesgirl in an
advertisement.
7 What should somebody do if they feel they are
being unfairly treated?

B   Vocabulary exercise

1 Other groups of people are *discriminated*
against, apart from women. Can you think of
some examples?
2 Imagine you were the manager of a shoe shop.
How would you set about *recruiting* new staff?
3 Think of some things which are *illegal* in most
countries.
4 You can *rent* a house or flat. Can you think of
some other things we might rent or hire?
5 Do you think *co-educational* schools are a good
idea? Give your reasons.
6 The new Act seeks to *eliminate* discrimination.
Teams and competitors can be eliminated in
sports competitions. Think of some examples.

C   Vocabulary exercise

For this exercise you may find an English-English
dictionary helpful. Each question begins with an
example from the Reading activity. In some
questions, all the answers might be correct. In
others, there are only one or two possible answers.

1   Landlords will be breaking the law if they do not provide the same opportunities and services. (line 4) Which of these could you *break?*
    a a promise
    b a contract
    c a habit
    d a heart

2   Employment agencies will not usually be able to label jobs 'for men' or 'for women'. (line 8) Which of these can be *labelled?*
    a a suitcase
    b a letter
    c a passport
    d a prescription

3   Banks, building societies and finance houses must not treat one sex less favourably than another. (line 27) Which of these could you *treat?*
    a a plant
    b a patient
    c a problem
    d a child

4   A job advertisement should make it clear that both men and women are eligible. (line 31) Which of these could you substitute for *clear?*
    a visible
    b obvious
    c distinct
    d understandable

5   Above all, the Commission will help you to know your rights and how to exercise them. (line 37) Which of these words could you substitute for *help?*
    a ease
    b assist
    c advise
    d accommodate

6   Advertisements may not indicate an intent to discriminate. (line 31) Which of these words could you use instead of *may?*
    a should
    b will
    c can
    d must

7   A job advertisement using terms such as 'waiter' should make it clear . . . (line 31) Which of these phrases could be used with *terms?*
    a of contract
    b of holiday
    c of payment
    d of imprisonment

D   Discussion

Do you have a sex discrimination act in your country?
If not, should you have one? Give your reasons.

The Act states that boys and girls should have equal opportunity in school. Think of any subjects you would be surprised to find (a) girls, (b) boys studying.

The Act aims to give equal opportunities to men and women. Yet men and women are different, aren't they? Do you believe there are some jobs that men do better than women and vice-versa? Make a list of them.

Can you think of any jobs which would definitely be:
(a) unsuitable for women?
(b) unsuitable for men?

Explain why.

E   Practice activity

Study these ideas:

After 29th December, any employer *will be breaking* the law if he/she discriminates against women.

After 29th December an employer *won't be allowed to* discriminate against women.

Even after 29th December schoolgirls *won't have to* play football or do mechanical drawing.

Imagine it is the year 2010. Oil is now in very short supply. The Government is going to pass some crazy new laws to ensure that petrol is not wasted. These laws will come into effect on 1st January.

1   Firms must use the railways to transport goods wherever possible.
2   Firms must not use trucks or lorries weighing more than 5 tons fully loaded.
3   Private motorists can only use their cars on a Saturday or Sunday.
4   Private motorists must carry at least one passenger for journeys of more than 20 miles.
5   Petrol stations are not to sell more than 2 gallons of petrol to private motorists on one day.

a Make up five sentences beginning 'After 29th December, X will be breaking the law if . . . '

b Now think of five things that firms, private motorists or petrol stations *won't be allowed to* do after 29th December.

c Think of one thing a big firm *won't have to* do and one thing private motorists *won't have to* do even *after* 29th December.

Discuss this point: When new laws are passed, people always look for loopholes, or ways round them.

If you were a private motorist, how would you get round the new situation?

F   Practice activity

Note this extract from the Reading activity:

Employers . . . will be breaking the law if they do not provide men and women with the same opportunities . . . (line 2)

The verb 'break' is frequently used with prepositions and adverbs. For example:

'Might I make a telephone call? Unfortunately my car's *broken down.*'
'Of course, help yourself.'

The air hostess who survived the crash *broke down* at the press conference when she was describing what happened.

The raiders *broke into* the workshop through a skylight and stole a number of expensive tools.

Baton-wielding policemen soon *broke up* the demonstration.

McCaffrey would never have *broken out of* prison without help from outside.
You may only use dead wood for the fire. You're not to *break* any branches *off* the trees.

Daniel Williams *broke off* in the middle of his speech and gazed at the ceiling. 'He's forgotten what he wants to say', whispered Ruth.

Replace the words in italics by suitable expressions with 'break'. Use each expression once only:

1 The woman *burst into tears* when she discovered that her handbag had been stolen.
2 Some of the prisoners-of-war tried to *escape from* the camp by digging a tunnel. But the guards discovered the tunnel.
3 The bus *stopped* at the traffic lights and the driver couldn't start the engine again. So there was a terrible traffic jam.
4 Somebody *entered the office illegally* and stole a number of important documents.
5 Political opponents of the 'Action Party' *ended* the meeting. Six people were taken to hospital.

G   Practice activity

George had only been a director of his father's firm for two years when the Sex Discrimination Act became law. He was explaining to his father how the changes would affect the firm:

'*Not only* will we now have to pay the girls equal pay for equal work, *but we'll* have to offer them equal opportunities for promotion too!'
'Good heavens,' said the old man, 'what's the world coming to?'

Look again at the text. Imagine you are explaining the effects of the new act to somebody who doesn't fully comprehend them. Make more remarks like George's with: 'Not only will . . . , but . . . too!' The note will help you:

1 girls be able to attend cookery classes/mechanical drawing classes
2 girls be able to become nurses/bus drivers
3 husbands be able to get a loan from the bank/wives
4 men be allowed a mortgage from a building society/women
5 employers be unable to discriminate against women/bank managers
6 banks have to be fairer to women in the future/insurance companies

UNIT 13   The right to be equal

Dialogue 🔘

Listen to this conversation in a busy office. There seem to be some problems. After you have listened, answer the impression questions.

H   Impression questions

1 How did Mr Clarke contact Dawn?
2 Why did Mr Clarke contact Dawn?
3 What do you think Mrs Freeman's job is?
4 What does Mr Clarke consider to be the most important qualification for his new employee?
5 How far away do you think a new employee is likely to live?
6 Why do you think Mr Clarke wanted to employ a single woman?
7 How do you think Mr Clarke feels about the new Sex Discrimination Act?
8 What must Mr Clarke leave out of his original advertisement?

I   Focus questions

As you learned in Unit 10, there are symbols in English that indicate words when messages are spoken or written in the form of a letter. Here is a copy of Mr Clarke's first suggestion for the advertisement.
'Wanted, receptionist for busy office. Single woman, 20–30. Typing essential.'

This is what Mr Clarke would say if he were speaking or writing a letter:
'We need a receptionist for our busy office. We prefer a single woman between 20 and 30. Typing is essential.'

Now study these advertisements. What would you say if you were speaking or writing a letter?

1 'Wanted, trainee mechanic for High Street garage. Man, 18–20. Experience not essential.'
2 'Shop assistant required for hotel florist. 5½ day week. £40 per week + bonus of 10% on sales.'
3 'For sale, mini cassette deck. 12″ × 5″ × 2″. Suitable bedsitter/small flat.'
4 'Sale beginning 7 January. Bargains in menswear. Shirts from £4.95. Knitwear from £6.95. Trousers from £8.99.'
5 'Carpet pieces for sale. All new. 5 × 4 yds—£25. 3 × 4 yds—£15. Various sizes/qualities. Can deliver.'

J   Discussion

The Sex Discrimination Act has caused a lot of people to think very carefully.

Imagine you are the manager of a hotel. You require:
1 Somebody to work in the bar at weekends.
2 A full-time waitress.

Remember Dawn's remarks to Mr C. If necessary, look again at the Reading activity. Then write two suitable advertisements.

Listening activity 🔘

K   Comprehension

Here are eight statements referring to Judy and Bob's conversation.
Decide if they are true or false.

1 Bob makes the assumption that Judy will be very pleased with the effects of the new act.
2 Judy is, in fact, quite pleased.
3 Judy thinks it is easier for a single woman to have a successful career than a married woman.
4 Bob believes that the decision about whether to have children or not is usually taken by the woman.

5 Judy disagrees with him about this.
6 Judy thinks that the wife loses more than the husband if there is a divorce.
7 Bob thinks the husband loses more than the wife if there is a divorce.
8 Bob is more pessimistic than Judy about the chance of a modern marriage being successful.

L   Gap dictation

Listen again to part of the conversation. Judy and Bob are discussing sex discrimination. Fill in the gaps in the discussion.

BOB   Oh, come on. Lots of successful career-women have children. (1)____ ____

JUDY   Yes, but (2)____ ____ ____, ____ ____. They have to take a few years off, so they (3)____ ____ ____ promotion opportunities. All the years the wife is at home (4)____ ____ ____ ____, the husband is (5)____ ____ his pension, but the woman (6)____ ____.

BOB   That doesn't really matter, (7)____ ____? After all, he's building up his pension (8)____ ____ ____ ____.

JUDY   Provided (9)____ ____ ____ ____ the marriage.

BOB   Oh, well, of course, there *is* the odd divorce.

JUDY   The chances of a marriage going wrong these days are (10)____ ____. And if it *does*, (11)____ ____?

M   Writing activity

Listen to the conversation again. Judy still believes that it's a man's world. Summarise her reasons for believing this.

N   Writing activity

Listen again to Bob and Judy talking about the position of women in English society.

Think about your country.

Has the position of women been greatly affected in your country by the Women's Liberation movement?
Is there anything you consider to be unfair about the position of women in your country? Write a composition of 250–350 words on: 'It's still a man's world'.

Summary

In this unit we compare and practise using the structures 'will be -ing', 'won't be allowed to', and 'won't have to'.

When the law regarding the wearing of seatbelts in cars has been passed, motorists:

will be breaking the law, if they don't wear a seatbelt.
won't be allowed to drive without a seatbelt.

However, passengers sitting in the back seat:

won't have to wear a seatbelt.

If you go to the zoo, you will be allowed to take photographs of the animals. Think of something you won't be allowed to do.

We also practise using constructions like this:
'*Not only* will we have to pay overtime, *but we'll have to* pay double time for the Saturday.'

Who do you think might make this remark? And who do you think he is talking to?

Note also these useful phrasal verbs with 'break':

break down, break into, break up, break out of, break off.

Why might a politician break off in the middle of his speech?

Why might a witness in a trial suddenly break down?

UNIT 14   Ghosts and spirits

Reading activity

COMMUNICATING WITH THE SPIRIT WORLD

1   It happened at an old inn in Barnard Castle. We were doing our military
service and celebrating the completion of a three-month gunnery course. As
the evening wore on, the talk turned to ghosts and the supernatural.

'It's the easiest thing in the world to communicate with the spirit world,'
5   remarked Jock Mackenzie.
'Rubbish,' replied Stan Turner. 'You've been reading too many Sunday
newspapers.'
'All right,' said Jock, 'I'll demonstrate.'

He persuaded the landlord to lend him a wine-glass, which he placed upside-
10   down in the centre of a highly-polished table. Then he wrote the letters of the
alphabet on small pieces of paper and placed them in no particular order
around the outside of the table. Then he put out the light at our end of the
room.
'Right,' he said. 'Put your fingers on the glass.'

15   Five of us sat down and did as we were instructed. Jock Mackenzie didn't sit
down with us. He stood by the table directing operations. At first nothing
happened. Then after some minutes the glass moved an inch or two. There
was much ribald laughter, accusations that so and so was cheating and a
certain amount of experimenting to see if it was in fact possible to push or
20   otherwise manoeuvre the glass towards a particular letter without the others
being aware that it was being done.

But gradually the glass seemed to become charged with an energy of its own. Its movements became more positive and some secret force appeared to direct it towards certain letters. It stopped by the H, then by the I, then by the Y.

25 'That's not a word,' said someone, 'let's start again.'

'OK,' said Jock, 'serious now. Start again.'

Once more the glass moved to the H, then to the I, then to the Y, then to the A, then to the B.

'It doesn't make sense,' said someone.

30 'Just keep going,' replied Jock.

The glass indicated the letter U, then the D.

'I say,' said someone incredulously, 'it does make sense, after all. "Hiya, bud". It must be an American spirit!'

Well, that glass kept moving round that table faster and faster, spelling out

35 answers to all sorts of ridiculous questions. Sometimes the answers seemed to make sense, other times they didn't. But whether the answers came from the spirit world or out of somebody's subconscious mind, I don't know to this day. I found the whole business pretty eerie. One thing I'm certain of. Nobody was pushing that glass.

A Questions

1 Why do you think the writer wore a uniform at one time?

2 Without looking at the text, describe how Jock prepared the table.

3 What did those taking part in the experiment have to do?

4 What happened when the glass first started moving about?

5 Why did someone say: 'It must be an American spirit'?

6 How did the writer feel about this experience?

B Vocabulary exercise

1 Assume that *ghosts* exist. Where would you expect to meet a ghost?

2 Make a list of the different ways in which people *communicate* with one another.

3 What sort of things might you see *demonstrated* in a big store?
You might also read about a political demonstration. What sort of things do people demonstrate about politically?

4 Can you think of some jobs in which people have to *persuade* other people to do things?

5 Think of some things that might be *highly polished*.

6 Think of some activities where people might be caught *cheating*.

7 What sort of people often carry out *experiments?*

8 Can you think of some really *ridiculous* excuses for turning up late for work?

C Vocabulary exercise

Here are five excerpts from the Reading activity. They are followed by a choice of answers. For some questions, all the answers might be correct. In others, only one or two could be used.

1 We were *doing* our military service. (line 1)
Which of these could you *do?*
a a job
b a mistake
c a decision
d a favour

2 'It's the easiest thing in the world to communicate with the spirit world,' *remarked* Jock Mackenzie. (line 4)
In this case, which of these words could you substitute for *remarked?*
a said
b told
c noticed
d observed

3 Five of us sat down and did as we were *instructed.* (line 15)
Which of these words could you substitute for *instructed* as used in the Reading activity?
a ordered
b told
c taught
d informed

4 He placed the small pieces of paper in no *particular* order. (line 11) Which of these words could replace *particular* in the Reading activity?
a special
b outstanding
c detailed
d definite

5 But gradually the glass seemed to become *charged* with an energy of its own. (line 22) The word *charged* has several meanings. Could it be used with the following words?
a a fee
b a jury
c a gun
d a battery

This is a word game. The words are POSITIVE ENERGY.

Rules:
1 Work with a group of at least four or five other students.
2 The words you find must be English words and must not be proper nouns.
3 Only the letters in POSITIVE ENERGY can be used. Do not use a letter more than once if it only occurs once. This applies to all the other letters.
4 Your teacher will tell you the time limit.

Here is an example:　YES (acceptable)
　　　　　　　　　　YOU (not acceptable; there is no U in POSITIVE ENERGY.)

Score 1 point for each letter in your words.

D　Discussion

Do you believe that this story is true?

What do you know about people's attempts to communicate with the spirit world?

Why do you think some people are very interested in this subject?

Would you like to be able to communicate with the spirits of people who have died?

Give your reasons.

If you could choose someone to communicate with, who would you choose?

E　Practice activity

In the text there are examples of the simple past:

Then he wrote the letters of the alphabet . . . (line 10)

and the past continuous:
We were doing our military service . . . (line 1)

Here is a letter from Stan Turner to his girl friend. In it Stan describes what happened. Put the verbs in brackets into the simple past or the past continuous.

Dear Pat,

I (get) two letters from you this morning, which (please) me very much. I (begin) to think you had forgotten all about me.

Last night we (have) a little party to celebrate the end of the course when something rather strange (happen). We (talk) about ghosts and things like that and Jock (say) he could show us how to communicate with the spirit world. Of course we all thought he (talk) rubbish. But he (borrow) a wine-glass and (place) it in the middle of the table. Then he (put) the letters of the alphabet round the ouside of the table and we all had to touch the glass with our fingers.

After a little while the glass (begin) to move from letter to letter. We (ask) questions and the glass (answer) them. I can't explain it at all, but I don't think anyone (push) the glass. It was very strange. I must stop now and polish my boots.

Much love,
Stan

F Practice activity

Stan Turner disagrees with Jock Mackenzie when he says it is easy to communicate with the spirit world, but they know one another quite well, so Stan isn't very polite. He says:
'Rubbish. You've been reading too many Sunday newspapers.'

If Stan had been talking to someone he didn't know so well, he might have said:
'Oh, I'm not sure about that,' or 'Do you really think so?'

If Stan had wanted to agree, he could have said:
'Yes, you're (quite) right.'

Work in pairs and agree or disagree with the following statements. Consider in each case who you're speaking to.

1 You're speaking to a very good friend. He says:
'Boxing is a marvellous sport. All little boys should learn to box.'
2 You're speaking to someone you have just met. She says:
'There's far too much pop music on the radio.'
3 You're speaking to a middle-aged man you don't know well. He says:
'They should have bigger classes in school and then education wouldn't be so expensive.'
4 You're speaking to a woman you don't know well. She says:
'Tinned fruit is much better for you than fresh fruit.'
5 You are speaking to a girl you know well. She says:
'Football is a ridiculous game.'
6 You are speaking to a stranger. She says:
'Japanese is a very easy language for foreigners to learn.'
7 You are speaking to a girl you have only just met. She says:
'Pop stars should earn a lot more money.'
8 You are speaking to a middle-aged man you don't know well. He says:
'Married women should stay at home and look after their husbands.'

G Practice activity

Jock *put out* the light at our end of the room. (line 12)

'Put' is often used with prepositions and adverbs.

For example:

She *put away* the cups and saucers.

He *put back* the records in the rack.

May I *put forward* a suggestion?

They *put off* the party because Emily was ill.

She *put on* her new blue dress.

The fishing boat *put out* a distress call.

We can *put you up* for the night.

I'm sorry you've got to share a room, but you'll just have to *put up with* it for a few days

Replace the words in italics by suitable expressions with 'put' from the list above. Use each expression once only.

1 We're *postponing* the picnic because of the weather.
2 He *got into* his blue jeans.
3 I'm sorry the weather is awful, but we'll just have to *endure* it for a few days.
4 She took the book from the shelf, glanced at it and *replaced* it.
5 Just after midnight the Captain *broadcast* an SOS message.
6 My sister can *offer you a bed* for a few days.
7 Robin listened carefully, then he *made* a suggestion 'Let's speak to Riley,' he said.

Dialogue 🔊

Stan and Jock are students at Southeast Shields
Polytechnic. They have decided to escape from
their engineering studies and get some fresh air and
exercise. After two days of hiking and camping in
wet, windy weather, they have agreed that it is time
for a little comfort.

Listen to Stan and Jock and answer the Impression
questions.

H   Impression questions

1   What do you think Jock meant by *that* and *this?*
2   Why do you think Stan was not very
    enthusiastic about the inn?
3   What do you think made the sounds that Stan
    heard?
4   Did Jock really think the sounds were made by
    a ghost?
5   Which of the two men was more nervous, Jock
    or Stan?
6   Does the painting of the ghost prove that the
    ghost really existed?
7   Why would the Museum of Costume be
    interested in a painting of a sixteenth century
    lady?
8   Do you think Stan believed Jock's story?
9   What were Jock's last five words?
10 What do you think they meant?

I   Focus questions

We often speak in incomplete sentences. For
example, Mr Freeman and Dawn would probably
have a short conversation like this:

MR FREEMAN   Busy, Dawn?
DAWN   Not really.

The full sentence would be:

MR FREEMAN   Are you busy, Dawn?
DAWN   I'm not really busy.

*Study these sentences from the Dialogue and say what
the full sentences would be. If you want to hear part of
the Dialogue again, ask your teacher to play it.*

1   JOCK   ... good to get out of that and into
               this ... A nice hot bath, and
               comfortable bed.

2   STAN   ... have their advantages, I suppose.
               Not sure I really like this place.

3   JOCK   Complaining? Lucky to find anywhere
               on a night like this.

4   JOCK   Probably the local ghost.

J   Discussion

What do you think of Jock's story?
Do you know anyone who claims to have seen a
ghost?
How would you react if you thought you saw a
ghost?
Would you be frightened?
If you don't believe in ghosts, how would you
explain all the stories about ghosts?
If you believe in ghosts, can you explain why there
are ghosts?

Ghosts and spirits

Listening activity 🔊

K Comprehension

Here are eight statements referring to the newspaper article. Decide whether they are true or false.

1 The police think someone has been behaving dishonestly.
2 Mr Took's mother lives in Beech Walk.
3 Mr Took told his mother about the advertisement in the paper.
4 Mr Took wasn't worried when his mother first started going to spiritualist meetings.
5 Mr Took's mother has been told to change her will.
6 A newspaper reporter had a conversation with Mr Stone.
7 Mr Stone says that he provides a great deal of comfort for lonely people.
8 Mr Stone agrees that he has been dishonest.

Here is the advertisement that Mr Took's mother saw in the newspaper.

Ancestry traced. Experienced genealogist. Less expensive than you think Tel. 489581

Dental repairs by qualified technician. Personal service. Tel. 874918

Ear piercing, painless and hygienic. Tel. 971849

Have you recently lost someone you love? We may be able to put you in touch. Contact the **Ringbourne Spiritualist Foundation** at once. Tel. 34271.

Social club. Why be lonely? Find friendship, love or marriage through our intoductions Tel. 554681.

Tarot cards or astrology. Madame Rosa. Tel. 628984.

Toupées, wigs, hairpieces, handmade to measure. Tel. 585186.

L Gap dictation

You are going to hear part of the Listening activity again. In the following newspaper account of investigations, certain key words and phrases are missing. Complete the account by writing the missing words.

Police (1)_____ investigating allegations of fraud (2)_____ _____ _____ spiritualist meetings (3)_____ _____ _____ _____ in a quiet Ringbourne road. The allegations (4)_____ _____ _____ by Mr Arthur Took, (5)_____ became alarmed when his mother, (6)_____ _____, began visiting the house in Beech Walk. 'My mother became very depressed after my father died two years ago, Mr Took told our reporter. 'She (7)_____ _____ _____ _____ _____ _____ _____ and began to attend spiritualist meetings. (8)_____ _____ I thought the meetings (9)_____ _____ _____ _____ a harmless interest, but I became alarmed when she started (10)_____

_____ _____ _____ _____ _____ _____

_____ _____, particularly when I realised that the messages (11)_____ _____ financial matters.

M Writing activity

Answer these questions. Write complete sentences.

1 What are the police investigating?
2 Who warned the police that something might be wrong?
3 When did Mr Took start getting worried?
4 What can you say about most of the people who attended the meetings?
5 What happened at the meetings?
6 What happened when Mr Took went to the meeting with his mother?
7 What did Mr Took's mother tell him afterwards?

N Writing activity

Now imagine you are writing an account of what happened to a friend in America. Tell the story and finish by giving *your* opinion of the 'Spiritualist Society'. You will need 200–250 words.

UNIT 14

Ghosts and spirits

Summary

In this unit we have further practice in using and contrasting the simple past tense with the past continuous.

Example: I *was doing* my military service when this incident *occurred*.
Why would it be wrong to use 'has occurred'?

We also practise agreeing and disagreeing politely and not so politely.

Example:
STAN   'Cricket is a much better game than football.'
ERNIE 'Rubbish. Cricket's slow and boring.'

How can you tell that Stan and Ernie know one another quite well?

How might Ernie have replied to Stan's remark if they had been comparative strangers?

Note these useful phrasal verbs with 'put': put out, put on, put away, put back, put forward, put off, put up, put up with.

Why might a football match be put off?

Think of some things you might have to put up with on a long railway journey in a very crowded train.

UNIT 15   The experience of being a twin

Reading activity

IDENTICAL TWINS

1   At the University of Minnesota, in the USA, scientists have been studying identical twins for more than 10 years and during this time they have come across many interesting cases. But recently they had a real stroke of luck. Previously, all the twins who had been investigated had been brought up
5   together, so it was difficult to pin-point the reasons for certain similarities. They might have been genetic, but they might just as well have been caused by the twins living in close proximity with one another.

   However, the two Jims were different. They were separated from one another and adopted by different families, called Lewis and Springer, a few weeks after
10   they were born and they did not meet again for 39 years. Eventually James Lewis, a security guard, of Lima, Ohio, approached the court which had arranged the adoptions and asked to be put in touch with his brother. It took a little while, but finally the court managed to trace James Springer. He was working as a records clerk in Dayton, Ohio.

15   When the scientists at Minnesota learnt about the two Jims, they were naturally invited to come to the University, where investigations revealed the most astonishing similarities in the pattern of their lives:

* Both married girls called Linda, were divorced and then married women called Betty.
20 * James Lewis named his first son James Alan. James Springer called his son James Allan.
* When they were boys, both owned dogs called Toy.
* Both had worked for the hamburger chain, McDonald's.
* Both had worked as attendants at filling stations.
25 * Both had the habit of biting their finger-nails.
* Both had Chevrolet cars and spent holidays at the same Florida seaside resort.
* They had similar sleeping problems and both suffered from migraine headaches which developed when they were 18.

30 How can one attempt to explain so many coincidences? Is it possible that twins have some mysterious way of communicating with one another at a subconscious level, so that an occurrence in the life of one twin is 'mirrored' in the life of the other? Or does our genetic make-up ensure that in certain circumstances we are bound to act in a certain way or take particular decisions?
35 At all events, it seems that many more aspects of our behaviour are influenced by genetic factors than we had previously imagined.

A Questions

1 What is the subject of the scientists' research?
2 What was the piece of good fortune the scientists enjoyed recently?
3 Explain exactly how the two Jims differed from other twins examined by the scientists.
4 Explain briefly how the two Jims got together again.
5 How many times has James Lewis been married?
6 Is there any suggestion in the passage that the twins might have consulted doctors? What about?
7 Do you know any way of discouraging a young person from biting his or her finger-nails?
8 Several coincidences are mentioned in the text. Can you find some of them?
9 The writer suggests two possible ways of explaining these coincidences. What are they?
10 What is the writer's conclusion?

B Vocabulary exercise

1 Twins can be *identical*. What other things could be identical?
2 Students taking an exam might have *a stroke of luck*. How?
3 Can you think of any situations in which a Member of Parliament might call for *'a full investigation'*?

4 Why might a lawyer wish to *trace* somebody?
5 Can you think of any *coincidences* you have heard about recently?
6 What sort of things might be described as *'mysterious'*?
7 Think of something you would like to buy, but about which you might say: *'It's bound to be expensive'*.
8 The word *'pattern'* is used in various contexts. Can you think of some of them?
9 Biting your finger-nails is a *bad habit*. Can you think of any more bad habits?
10 *'Reveal'* is a verb. The noun is 'revelation'. If a popular Sunday newspaper promised to make revelations about some famous person, what sort of facts would you expect to discover?

C Vocabulary exercise

Here are five excerpts from the Reading activity. They are followed by a choice of answers. For some questions, all the answers might be correct. For others, only one or two could be used.

1 But recently they had a stroke of luck. (line 3) Which of these words could be used with the phrase *a stroke of?*
a work
b business
c genius
d lightning

2 Previously, all the twins who had been investigated had been brought up together. (line 4) Which of these could be *investigated?*
a an accident
b a complaint
c a patient
d a crime

3 It was difficult to pin-point the reason for certain similarities. (line 5) Which of these words could you substitute for *certain?*
a reliable
b sure
c particular
d some

4 Eventually, James Lewis approached the court which had arranged the adoptions. (line 10) Which of these words could be used instead of *eventually?*
a finally
b in the end
c at the end
d at last

5 When the scientists at Minnesota learned about the two Jims, they were naturally invited to come to the University. (line 15) Which of these words and phrases could be used to replace *naturally?*
a normally
b easily
c of course
d usually

D Vocabulary exercise

Read these five incomplete sentences. Then study the Reading activity and find words or phrases that could complete the sentences.

1 TEACHER Oranges and lemons are _____ but not _____. What is the difference?

2 SECRETARY I haven't managed to _____ your application. Perhaps it wasn't addressed properly.

3 HUSBAND I finally arrived at the meeting when all the others were leaving. I might _____ _____ _____ have stayed at home.

E Discussion

Do you think twins have some mysterious way of communicating with one another?

In what ways do people communicate with one another, apart from speaking?

Think about your friends. Why do you think we become more friendly with some people than others – is it shared interests, or a similar background, or a similar view of life?

It has been suggested that opposites attract each other. What is your opinion?

F Practice activity

In the text there are examples of the simple present:
Is it possible that twins have some mysterious way of communicating . . . ? (line 30)

the simple past:
Eventually James Lewis . . . approached the court . . . (line 10)

and the present perfect continuous:
. . . scientists have been studying identical twins . . . (line 1)

Here is a letter that one Jim might have written to his twin brother. Put the verbs in brackets into the simple present, the simple past or the present perfect continuous.

Dear Jim,

It was great to get your letter. As you know I live in Lima, Ohio. My family (move) here when I was still a kid, so I (think) of Lima as my home town.

When I left school I (get) a job with McDonald's, the hamburger people, but I only (stay) there for a year or so. After that I (work) at a filling station for a few years. Then I (spend) some time on the assembly line at a canning factory. But after a while I (find) the work very boring and I (want) a change.

For the past eight years I (work) as a security guard. The pay is not bad and every day is a little different.

When I was 25 I (marry) a girl called Linda, but unfortunately this marriage was not a success and we were divorced three years later. However, a short while afterwards I (meet) Betty. We got married and we (have) two sons aged 9 and 7.

I am looking forward to meeting you and finding out what you (do) during the last 39 years. I hope life (treat) you well.

Yours very sincerely,
Jim

G   Practice activity

Study this pattern:

Perhaps the reasons for the similarities were genetic.
The reasons for the similaritities *might have been* genetic.

Use *might have* . . . in the following situations:

1. Perhaps Toy was a very common name for a dog.
2. Perhaps the Chevrolet was a very popular make of car at that time.
3. Perhaps it was easy to get a job at McDonald's.
4. Perhaps they had sleeping problems because they were twins and twins don't like being separated.
5. Perhaps they had good maths teachers, who interested them in the subject.
6. Perhaps biting their nails was a nervous habit.
7. Perhaps Florida was the most natural place to go for a holiday.
8. Perhaps their mother or father had similar migraine headaches.

H   Practice activity

Note these two extracts from the Reading activity:

. . . all the twins . . . had been *brought up* together. (line 4)
. . . they have *come across* many interesting cases. (line 2)

The verbs 'come' and 'bring' are frequently used with prepositions and adverbs. For example:

He was *brought up* in the United States.

I would rather you didn't *bring up* the subject of money at the meeting.

I'll *bring round* that recipe this evening.

In cowboy films, when there is a fight and someone is knocked out, they usually *bring him round* by throwing a bucket of water over him.

We do not hang criminals now, but whenever there is a nasty murder people say 'they should *bring back* hanging'.

The football team from the Third Division *brought off* a surprise win.

I *came across* this pretty porcelain jug in an antique shop in Brighton.

A strange feeling *came over* him.

His wicked plan didn't *come off*.

He tripped and fell and hit his head on a stone. When he *came round*, it was quite dark.

Replace the words in italics by suitable expressions with 'come' or 'bring' from the list above. Use each expression once only.

1. He thinks they ought to *re-introduce* corporal punishment in schools.
2. Coles *won* a remarkable victory in the final of the tennis tournament.
3. Paul heard a sound behind him. As he turned, some heavy object hit the side of his head and everything went black. When he *recovered consciousness*, the house was silent.
4. I'm sure Smith will *raise* the question of staff holidays at the meeting.
5. Where did you *find* this little oil-painting?
6. Frederick intended to marry the daughter of extremely rich parents, but his scheme didn't *succeed*. She married his best friend instead.

The experience of being a twin UNIT 15

Dialogue 🔊

The World of Investigation can be seen on Wednesday evenings. The current investigation involves twins and their similarities and differences. Laura X, an identical twin, has agreed to be interviewed.

Read the Impression questions. Then listen to the Dialogue.

I   Impression questions

1   What do you think is the difference between 'apologising' and 'feeling sorry'?
2   Why do you think Laura made a distinction between 'sisters' and 'identical twins'?
3   Was Laura's mother happy to have twins?
4   Why do you think Laura and Sarah have always dressed alike?
5   Laura giggled and changed the subject. Why, do you think?
6   The interviewer then changed the subject. Why, do you think?
7   How would you describe Laura?
8   How would you describe Sarah?
9   How many questions were not answered?
10   What do you think Laura's main point was?

J   Focus questions

One of the typical features of English is the use of negative or leading questions to get more information. Here is an example from the dialogue.

INTERVIEWER	Don't you think there are quite a few sisters who aren't close?
DIRECT QUESTION	Do you think there are sisters who aren't close?

Evening TV Guide

6.03   News and Weather
6.20   Sportscall
6.30   Today in London
7.00   Love Calling
→ **7.30**   The World of Investigation
8.30   Men and Machines
8.45   Big Bill
9.00   News

Listen to the Dialogue again and find three more examples of negative or leading questions. Then say what the direct question would be.

1   INTERVIEWER   _____
    DIRECT
    QUESTION   _____

2   INTERVIEWER   _____
    DIRECT
    QUESTION   _____

3   INTERVIEWER   _____
    DIRECT
    QUESTION   _____

K   Discussion

Have you ever known any identical twins?
What can you remember about them?
Were they closer than ordinary brothers and sisters? In what ways?
Do you have any brothers or sisters?
How old are they?
Do you feel close to them?
Do you feel that you come closer to brothers and sisters as you get older? Give your reasons.

The experience of being a twin

Listening activity 🔊

L Comprehension

Here are eight statements referring to Alan and Barbara's conversation. Decide whether they are true or false.

1 Alan and Barbara agree that criminals are born and not made.
2 Barbara suggests that there are families that don't like the police.
3 Alan suggests that thieves sometimes tell the police about one another.
4 Alan suggests that all policemen and all criminals have the same qualities.
5 Barbara accuses Alan of being unfair to policemen.
6 Alan says that men who might be criminals in peacetime often make brave soldiers when there is a war on.
7 Alan says that in time of war prisoners are taken out of jail so that they can become soldiers.
8 Alan says that some criminals get bored with ordinary everyday life.

M Gap dictation

You are going to hear part of the Listening comprehension again. Certain words and phrases are missing and the meaning is incomplete. Write the missing words and phrases and complete the meaning.

ALAN   That idea about our genetic make-up (1)_____ _____ _____, isn't it?
BARBARA Do you mean the idea (2)_____ _____ _____ our genetic make-up we

(3)_____ _____ _____ _____ in a particular way?
ALAN   Yes. If it's true, (4)_____ _____ _____ _____ criminals are born and not made.
BARBARA Not necessarily. It would only mean that somebody (5)_____ _____ _____ the potential (6)_____ _____ a criminal.
ALAN   (7)_____ _____ _____ _____?
BARBARA Well, if (8)_____ was born with a particular set of genes (9)_____ _____ _____ a potential criminal, it would be necessary for him to be brought up in a particular way if he was actually going to become a criminal.
ALAN   (10)_____ _____ _____ _____ _____ in a family of criminals, you mean?

N Writing activity

Listen to Alan and Barbara's conversation again. Summarise Alan and Barbara's arguments.

O Writing activity

Alan and Barbara have raised some interesting points in their discussion, but they haven't said everything, have they? What about friends, for example? Sometimes our friends have more influence over us than our families.
Make a list of the influences that have been important in your life. Then write a paragraph of about 200 words to describe these influences and their effects.

Summary

In this unit we compare the use of the simple present tense with that of the simple past and the present perfect continuous.

Here is an example of the present perfect continuous tense:
Rosemary wants to become a doctor. She *has been studying* hard for the last five years.

Can you explain when we need to use this tense?

We also practise using 'might have'.

Example:
TOM   'Why do you think the two Jims both worked at filling stations?'

PETER   'It *might have been* very easy to get that sort of job because there were so many filling stations near where they lived.'

Could you take Peter's part and reply to Tom without using 'might have'?

Note also these useful phrasal verbs with 'bring' and 'come': bring up, bring round, bring back, bring off, come across, come over, come off, come round.
What might an unfashionable football team bring off?
In what circumstances might an art dealer come across a valuable painting?

UNIT 16 Making decisions

Reading activity

PARKINSON'S LAW

1   The slim volume entitled *Parkinson's Law or the Pursuit of Progress* by
C. Northcote Parkinson should be required reading for all civil servants and
administrators.

    'Work expands so as to fill the time available for its completion,' Parkinson
5 tells us, and he goes on to show that the more people who are employed on a
task, the more important that task will appear to become and thus the more
time will be spent upon it.

    Parkinson deals with 'The short list or principles of selections,' 'The annual
general meeting' and 'How to spot the really important people at a cocktail
10 party'. But perhaps the most thought-provoking chapter is the one devoted to
the workings of the finance committee.

    Parkinson suggests that the time spent in discussing items on the agenda will
vary according to the amount of money involved. One might assume that
major items of expenditure would be discussed at length, while those
15 involving smaller amounts would be summarily dealt with.

    However, Parkinson puts forward the theory that so few members of the
committee will have the knowledge necessary to discuss really large items that

these are likely to be approved with little or no discussion, while quite small matters, readily comprehensible to all the members, will provoke fierce
20   argument and take much longer to settle.

He quotes the example of a finance committee called upon to approve the spending of 10 million pounds upon a new atomic reactor. Of the 11-man committee, only two have the slightest idea of how much it should cost. As a result, the expenditure is agreed to inside three minutes. However, an
25   estimate of £350 for the building of a new bicycle shed for the use of the clerical staff is a matter on which all the members of the committee feel able to comment. As a result, 45 minutes are spent discussing this item.

A review of *Parkinson's Law* in the *Financial Times* contained these words: 'A devilish book. No businessman should let it fall into the hands of his staff.'

A   Questions

1   Why do you think the writer recommends that all administrators and civil servants should read *Parkinson's Law?*
2   Can you explain what the short list is? When is it used?
3   Which chapter in the book is most likely to cause readers to think deeply?
4   Why does Parkinson think it might be easier to persuade a finance committee to spend a large amount of money than a small amount?
5   Why do you think a businessman might be sorry if his staff got a copy of *Parkinson's Law?*
6   Do you think the *Financial Times* reviewer was completely serious?

B   Vocabulary exercise

1   *'Pursuit'* is a noun. 'Pursuit' is the verb. What sort of people might be pursued by photographers?
2   Suggest three items which might be on the *agenda* of the Annual General Meeting of a sports club.
3   Is there any special place in your home country where you might *spot* famous people? Where?
4   We can say: 'The weather *varies* from day to day in England.' Think of some other things that might vary from time to time.
5   If you heard someone say: 'It was a very unpleasant *task*', what do you think they might be referring to?
6   Can you think of any remarks a person might make which would probably *provoke* an argument?

C   Vocabulary exercise

Here are eight excerpts from the Reading activity. They are followed by a choice of answers. For some questions, all the answers might be correct. For others, only one or two could be used.

1   The slim volume should be required reading. (line 1) Which of these words could be substituted for *slim* in this case?
  a   thin
  b   small
  c   slight
  d   slender

2   The more people who are employed on a task, the more important that task will appear. (line 5) Which of these words could you use instead of *appear?*
  a   arrive
  b   pretend
  c   seem
  d   come

3   Parkinson deals with 'The short list, or principles of selection'. (line 8) In this example, which words could replace *principles?*
  a   rules
  b   laws
  c   morals
  d   truths

4   Parkinson suggests that the time spent in discussing items on the agenda will vary. (line 12) Which of these words could be used in place of *suggests?*

a recommends
b proposes
c argues
d insists

5 It might be assumed that major items of expenditure would be discussed at length. (line 13) Which of these phrases could replace *at length?*
a at last
b for long
c in detail
d in full

6 Quite small matters will provoke fierce argument. (line 18) Find any words that could replace *argument* in this example.
a disagreement
b discussion
c debate
d conversation

7 However, an estimate of £350 for the building of a new bicycle shed for the use of clerical staff . . . (line 24) Which of these words could replace *however?*
a Because
b Nevertheless
c Although
d In spite

8 A review of *Parkinson's Law* in the *Financial Times* contained these words: 'A devilish book.' (line 28) Which of these words could be used instead of *review?*
a examination
b account
c criticism
d report

D Discussion

'Work expands so as to fill the time available for its completion.'

Here is an example:

Two men are given the job of painting a large hall, and five days are allocated for the job. The men start on the ceiling and work very hard for the first two days. If the job is nearly finished by the end of the third day, they will probably be quite happy to spend the fourth and fifth days finishing off the job. It is unlikely that they will say to their boss: 'We can finish this job in four days'!

Can you think of another real-life situation like this?

E Practice activity

It is often difficult to decide when to use the 'going to' future and when to use 'will'. Usually it depends upon the speaker's attitude. Remember that we often use the 'going to' form to express the idea that the subject has deliberately chosen the course of action to be followed, while the use of 'will' implies simply that the action is likely to occur. Occasionally where there is a choice, one or other form may be chosen on stylistic grounds.

The chairman of the company has written a letter to inform all personnel of certain decisions that have been taken by the board. If you were the chairman, would you use 'should', 'is/are going to' or 'will' in the gaps in the letter? Indicate where there is more than one possibility.

Explain why you have chosen the answers you have.

Ladies and Gentlemen,

It is unnecessary for me to tell you that these are difficult days for our company. In the present economic climate it is very difficult to make long-term plans with any certainty that they (1)_____ come to fruition. It is apparent that our present operation is too large and we (2)_____ have to carry out a certain amount of re-organisation. We (3)_____ close our North End factory and we (4)_____ (also) reduce our workforce at Ford End Road by approximately 30 per cent. There is no doubt this (5)_____ mean that there (6)_____ be redundancies amongst our employees, but it is my personal wish that these (7)_____ be voluntary wherever possible. In addition we (8)_____ introduce a new early retirement scheme which (9)_____ come into effect immediately. The new scheme includes an offer of extremely generous redundancy payments and other incentives. If you are aged 55 or over, you (10)_____ consider this new scheme most carefully.

I greatly regret that it is necessary to take these steps.

N.J. Binns
Chairman

F   Practice activity

Note these extracts from the Reading activity:

. . . a finance committee *called upon* to approve the spending of £10 million. (line 21)
No businessman should let it *fall into* the hands of his staff. (line 29)

The verbs 'call' and 'fall' are frequently used with prepositions and adverbs. For example:

It used to be the custom to *call on* new neighbours and leave your card, but people are too busy for that sort of thing now.

They had to *call off* the football match, because the pitch was covered in snow.

The local police couldn't solve the murder, so they *called in* Scotland Yard.

I'll *call for* you about 6 o'clock tomorrow evening.

'What's the matter with your leg?'
'You won't believe this, but I *fell off* a camel.'

There is a lot of unemployment in the town. It was hoped that the Ford company might build a new factory here, but the deal *fell through*.

The suitcase burst open and hundreds of new pound notes *fell out*.

Tom and Susan were happy till Tom won the money. Then they *fell out* over how it should be spent.

Replace the words in italics by suitable expressions with 'call' or 'fall'. Use each expression once only.

1 There isn't going to be a party after all. Henry wanted to hire a hall but the plan *failed* when we discovered how expensive it would be.
2 Rose *visited* the people next door and told them about the club.
3 The concert *was cancelled* because only 15 tickets had been sold.
4 After their father died, the brothers *quarrelled* over the will.
5 I'm sorry I'm late. Frank promised to *fetch* me, but he forgot, so I had to come by bus.

G   Practice activity

Imagine you are the manager of a small business. Your staff have just read Parkinson's 'devilish' book and as a result keep criticising your decisions.

You might say: I wish you *wouldn't* keep criticising my decisions.
or   I wish you *hadn't* read that wretched book.

We use: 'I wish you would (do) . . .' and 'I wish you wouldn't (do) . . .' to express annoyance, polite complaint or even encouragement about somebody's present or general behaviour or actions. For example:

I wish you wouldn't make so much noise.
I wish you wouldn't expect me to solve all your problems.
I wish you would get up on time.
I wish you would have a bit more confidence in yourself.

We use 'I wish you had (done) . . .' and 'I wish you hadn't (done) . . .' to express regret, or reproach after somebody has done something you don't like.

Examples: I wish you had remembered to send Ilse a birthday card. (You didn't send a card and I'm sorry about it.)
I wish you hadn't lost your temper with Meg. (You lost your temper with Meg and I'm sorry about it.)

Practise using 'I wish you would/wouldn't/had/hadn't . . .'.

1 Your friend Sonia got married. You aren't happy about this. Tell her so.
2 Don *could* come and work for the same firm as you, but he isn't going to. You're sorry about this. Tell him how you feel.
3 A friend of yours used to have a beautiful piano, but she sold it. You are sorry that she sold it. Tell her.
4 Rosemary has said she can't come to the party on Saturday, but you think she might change her mind. Try and persuade her.
5 Frank has a habit of making noises with his fingers which annoys you. Tell him how you feel.
6 Robert borrowed a book from you. You've asked him for it back twice, but he keeps making excuses. Tell him how you feel.
7 When your friend Gladys makes the coffee, she always makes it very strong. You don't like your coffee too strong. What could you say to Gladys?
8 Your friend Steve has just come to see you. It is 12.30 on a Sunday. If you'd known he was coming, you'd have prepared a nice meal. What do you say to him?

Making decisions

Dialogue 🔘

Ted Park is a rather unhappy young man. He has just spent four years at university but he can't find a job. He has sent in a great many applications and has had a lot of polite letters of refusal. He is living in his parents' house. Listen to this conversation and answer the Impression questions.

H   Impression questions

1 Who spoke to Ted?
2 Why did she shout?
3 What do you think Ted was doing when she came in?
4 Do you think his mother was excited about going to the party?
5 What time do you think Ted's parents will get to the party?
6 Who has invited them to the party?
7 How do you think Ted feels about the party? Would he like to go?
8 Why do you think Ted is quoting Parkinson?
9 Do you think Ted's father and mother really want to go to the party?
10 What do you think Ted will do while his parents are out?

I   Focus questions

Ted stressed certain words during his conversation. His mother knew exactly what he meant. Do you? Here is an example. Listen again.

TED   Where are *you* going?
Ted was surprised. Was his mother pleased?
Ted thought his mother was looking unusually attractive. His mother was very pleased.

Now mark the stress on the most important words and say what these words mean when they are stressed.

1	TED	You should read it.
	MARJORIE	Why should I read it?
2	MARJORIE	By their clothes, I suppose?
	TED	No, not their clothes.
3	TED	That's interesting.
4	TED	Just as I thought. You are important guests.
5	MARJORIE	What does Parkinson know about us?
	TED	Nothing about you as individuals. Quite a lot about you as types.

J   Discussion

Name five people that you think are important.

Do you think important people behave differently from other people?

How do they behave?

Are they usually polite to waitresses, or shop assistants?

Do you think they are more careful about what time they arrive at a function than other people?

Do important people dress in a particular way? What sort of clothes do they wear?

Do you express your personality through the clothes you wear? Try and give one or two examples.

What do you think about the idea that people keep away from the centre of the room?

Where would you sit if you entered an empty restaurant?

Listening activity 🔘

K   Comprehension

Here are seven statements referring to the
conversation between Elena and Eddie. Decide
whether they are true or false:

1   Eddie considers the British system of choosing
     a parliament to be fair.
2   Eddie is surprised by Elena's suggestion that
     the British system is not absolutely fair to
     everyone.
3   Eddie says that the minority parties have a
     chance of winning an election.
4   Elena believes that people are silly to vote for
     minority parties.
5   Elena and Eddie disagree as to whether votes
     for minority parties are wasted votes.
6   Eddie does not think that coalition
     governments are a good idea.
7   Eddie concedes that Elena may be right.

L   Gap dictation

You are going to hear part of the Listening activity
again. Certain words and phrases are missing, so
the meaning is incomplete. Write the missing
words and phrases and complete the meaning.

EDDIE   Undemocratic? Of course not. One
          person, one vote, a secret ballot. And
          every member of parliament (1)_____
          _____ _____ by a majority of the

(2)_____ _____ _____.

ELENA   (3)_____ _____ the minority parties?
EDDIE   Well, everybody (4)_____ _____,
          _____ _____?
ELENA   Of course not. But with your system,
          (5)_____ _____ _____ could vote for a
          minority party. But (6)_____ _____
          _____ _____ _____ _____
          _____, their votes are wasted.
EDDIE   Their votes aren't wasted. (7)_____
          _____ _____ _____.
ELENA   Of course they're wasted. In Italy we have
          proportional representation. All the votes
          (8)_____ _____ _____ and each party
          (9)_____ _____ according to how many
          people voted for them.

M   Writing activity

Listen to the conversation again. Summarise the
points made by Elena and Eddie.

N   Writing activity

One chapter of Parkinson's book is concerned with
the 'The short list or principles of selection', i.e.,
choosing the right person for the job.

Discuss the qualities required by somebody in a
position of authority.

Then write 200–250 words on 'A good boss'.

Summary

In this unit we practise using 'should' and compare
the 'going to' future with the simple future.

Examples:
'There *will* unfortunately *be* further redundancies.
We *are*, however, *going to* introduce a generous
early retirement scheme, which *should prove*
attractive to older members of our workforce.'

What expression could be used instead of 'should'
in the above example?

We also compare the use of 'I wish you
would/wouldn't' with 'I wish you had/hadn't'.

Examples:
I wish you would get another job.
I wish you wouldn't spend so much money on
records.
I wish you had told me about this before.
I wish you hadn't kept this to yourself.

When do we use 'I wish you hadn't . . .'?

Note also these useful phrasal verbs with 'call' and
'fall':
call on, call off, call for, call in, fall off, fall through,
fall out.

What might cause a business deal to fall through?
Why might a ski race be called off?

UNIT 17 Remembering and forgetting

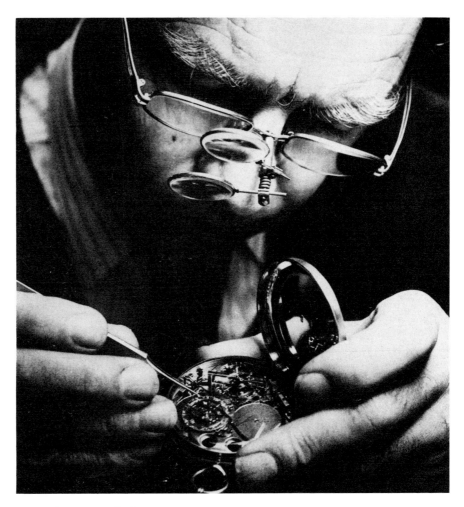

Reading activity

I NEVER FORGET A NAME

1 When I left school, I went to work for Mr Humphries. He had an old-
established jewellery business in my home town of Bedford. I wasn't being
trained as a skilled craftsman, you must understand, I was simply a junior
shop assistant. If customers brought in a watch or a clock for repair I would
5 take it upstairs to the watchmaker for an estimate, inform the customer of the
likely cost and issue a repair ticket. At the same time I was allowed to sell small
items, but whenever customers wished to purchase anything exceeding £10 in
value, I was instructed to pass them over to Humphries himself.

One day, a clergyman called to see Humphries. He was a slightly-built, grey-
10 haired man, with a pale, lined face and a small, petulant mouth. Humphries
wasn't in that day, so I asked if I could help. Reluctantly the clergyman
produced a gold watch which he wished to have repaired.
'Would you like an estimate?' I asked.

'That won't be necessary,' he told me. So I gave him a repair ticket and the
15   watch was taken to the watchmaker in the usual way.

Ten days later the clergyman returned. Again he asked for Mr Humphries and
again Humphries was out.
'I'll see if your watch is ready, sir,' I said.

It was. 'It's been cleaned and overhauled,' I told him. '£2.50, please.'
20   'Rubbish, young man,' said the clergyman, 'I'm an old friend of Mr
Humphries and he never charges me for my repairs.'
'I'm very sorry,' I replied angrily, 'but I know nothing about that. You'd better
come back this afternoon and see Mr Humphries personally.'
He went out, slamming the shop door behind him.

25   When Mr Humphries came in, I told him what had happened. He was not
pleased.
'You should have informed me as soon as the watch was brought in,' he said
testily. 'You take too much responsibility upon yourself.'

I worked for Humphries for nearly seven years, and from time to time the
30   clergyman would come in with something to be repaired, and I could never
remember his name. Then one day I borrowed a book by Sigmund Freud
from the library. Freud believed that forgetting things can sometimes be a
defence mechanism, and suddenly I realised. I took a plain piece of paper and
a pencil and began to write:

35   watch . . . gold . . . round . . . hands . . . feet . . . shoes . . . leather . . . cows . . .
field . . . tree . . . willow . . . beech . . . a beech tree . . . the Reverend Beech.

I never forgot his name again.

A   Questions

1   Why was it necessary to give customers an estimate for the repair of their watches?
2   Did the writer sell many expensive diamond rings?
3   Why was the clergyman reluctant to show his watch to the writer?
4   How did the clergyman express his irritation?
5   What was Mr Humphries' reaction to what had happened?
6   Where did the writer get the book by Freud?

B   Vocabulary exercise

1   Humphries had a *jewellery* business. What sort of things do you think were sold in his shop?
2   The watchmaker was a *skilled craftsman.* Can you think of any other businesses where you might find skilled craftsmen working? What do they do?

3   Have you made any interesting *purchases* in the last few days? Tell us about them.
4   Would you expect a boxer to be *slightly built?* Give your reasons.
5   The clergyman wished *to have his watch repaired.* Think of something else he might wish to have repaired. Can you think of anything a person might wish to have cleaned?
6   If you bought a suit and the trousers were too long, would you expect to be *charged* for having them shortened? Give your reasons.
7   When did you last *slam* a door? Why did you slam it?
8   What was the last thing you *borrowed?* Have you lent anything to anybody recently?

C   Vocabulary exercise

Here are eight excerpts from the Reading activity. Without looking at the text, find the prepositions or adverbs that could be used to complete each excerpt.

1   When I left school, I went _____ work _____ Mr Humphries.

2   I wasn't being trained _____ a skilled craftsman, you must understand.

3   If customers brought _____ a watch for repair, I would take it _____ the watchmaker _____ an estimate and inform the customer _____ the likely cost.

4   Ten days later, the clergyman returned. Again he asked _____ Mr Humphries.

5   'I'm an old friend _____ Mr Humphries', said the clergyman.

6   'I know nothing _____ that,' I replied angrily.

7   I worked for Humphries for nearly seven years and _____ time _____ time the clergyman would come in _____ something to be repaired.

8   Then one day I borrowed a book _____ Sigmund Freud _____ the library.

D   Discussion

Apparently the writer continually forgot the name of the clergyman because, deep down, he didn't want to remember his name.

Can you explain why he didn't want to remember his name?

Have you ever found yourself mysteriously forgetting the name of somebody or something? Why do you think it happened?

Do you believe it is possible to recall things you find difficult to remember by using a system like this?

How do you remember important dates and facts?

E   Practice activity

Mr Humphries said:
You *should have informed* me as soon as the watch was brought in.'

He could also have said:
'You *shouldn't have charged* him without asking me first.'

Here are some more situations. Practise using 'should have' and 'shouldn't have'.

1   The young man accepted a watch for cleaning and quoted a price of £2.50. The customer left the shop. When the watchmaker took off the back of the watch, he found that it had been dropped and badly damaged. The watchmaker said to the young man: _____

2   A customer took some shoes to be repaired. He was told they would be ready in a fortnight. Three weeks later they were still not ready. What do you think the customer said?

3   You are driving along with a friend in your car and your friend notices that your petrol gauge shows that you have very little petrol. You pass a petrol station and your friend suggests stopping to fill up. You say the petrol gauge isn't working. Five minutes later, you run out of petrol. What do you think your friend will say?

4   A friend borrowed your car without asking, and bumped into another car at the traffic lights. What would you say to him?

5   Your friend Ronald, who is very unfit, was persuaded to take part in a football match. He had to come off the field after 25 minutes and is now suffering from very bad cramp. You say to him: _____

Think of some more situations where the phrase 'should have' or the negative form 'shouldn't have' would be useful.

F   Practice activity

Note this extract from the Reading activity:

Reluctantly, the clergyman produced a gold watch, which he wished to have repaired. (line 11)

We use the 'to have something done' construction when somebody else is going to do something for us.

For instance, if the electric wiring in your house needs replacing you would say: *'I'm going to have the house re-wired.'*

If you buy a second-hand car, you might decide to have it re-sprayed. Then you could say to a friend: *'I want to have the car re-sprayed.'*

Here are some more common 'have something done' situations:

We might have a specially good photograph *enlarged.*
Before we can insure an item of jewellery, we must have it *valued.*

We have a car *serviced* from time to time.
We have a bad tooth *filled* or *taken out*.
We can have a tennis racquet *re-strung*.
We have a film *developed*.
We have a tear in a jacket *invisibly mended*.
When a suit is dirty, we have it *dry-cleaned*.

What would you say in the following circumstances?
Use expressions from the examples above:

1   Your friend has a smart suit, but it has a number of stains on the front. You give this advice to your friend: (should)
2   You decide to insure your pearl necklace. You take it to a jeweller's shop and say: (I'd like)
3   In a few days you are going on a long journey by car. You say to a friend: (must)
4   Your friend has been complaining of toothache for several days. Give her some good advice: (should)
5   You've taken all the photographs on the film. You remove the film from your camera and say to a friend: (want)
6   When you see the photographs, you find that one of the pictures is exceptionally good. You take the negative back to the shop and say: (I'd like)
7   You tore your jacket on a barbed-wire fence. You take it to the shop and you say: (I'd like)
8   The strings of your tennis racquet are becoming very loose and one is broken, but the frame is still in good condition. You take it to the sports shop and you say: (I'd like)

G   Practice activity

Note these extracts from the Reading activity:

. . . I was instructed to *pass* them over to Humphries . . . (line 8)
So I *gave* him a repair ticket . . . (line 14)

The verbs 'pass' and 'give' are frequently used with prepositions and adverbs. For example:

He took two aspirins and after a while the headache *passed off*.

When Moira saw the hypodermic syringe in the doctor's hand she *passed out*.

He could have gone to university but he *passed up* the opportunity.

Dawn won the box of chocolates in the raffle, but as she was trying to slim, she *gave them away*.

The news of the kidnapping was *given out* on the radio.

Burning rubber *gives off* a terrible smell.

Excuse me, I think you forgot to *give me back* my tennis racquet.

When they saw that they were surrounded, the rebels *gave up*.

Pat *gave up* smoking two years ago, but David still smokes like a chimney.

We shall never *give in* to blackmail . . .

Replace the words in italics by suitable expressions with 'pass' or 'give'. Use each expression once only:

1   He didn't *stop* playing football till he was over forty.
2   Although West Ham attacked constantly, the Spurs defence refused *to surrender,* and five minutes from time Hoddle broke away on the right and Ardiles scored the winner.
3   I must *return* the books I borrowed.
4   The news that Rodrigo's car was a non-starter was *announced* over the loudspeakers.
5   For several days he felt depressed, but as the weather improved, his depression *lifted*.
6   As soon as Donaldson saw the blood he *fainted*.

Dialogue 📼

Before you listen to the dialogue, read the Impression questions. This will help you to concentrate on the information you need.

H   Impression questions

1   Do you think Gwen and Tony are old friends? What gives you this impression?
2   Why do you think Colin said, 'Excuse me, are you a psychology professor?'
3   How would you describe Gwen's reaction to his question?
4   How recently had Gwen and Colin met?
5   Why do you think Colin was surprised when he saw that Gwen was reading a book about dreams?
6   What was Colin trying to explain?
7   What do you think he was really doing in France?
8   How much do you think Gwen has found out about dreams?
9   Why do you think the boy in Colin's story was looking so miserable?
10   What do you think 'a nightmare' is?

Now listen to the Dialogue. Ask your teacher to repeat it when you need more information. Then answer the Impression questions.

I   Focus questions

Colin told Gwen a very amusing story. Imagine the actual conversation between and Colin and his pupil and write exactly what they said. Here is an example:

Colin had told Jean-Luc that he wanted him to dream in English.
COLIN   Jean-Luc, I want you to dream in English.

1   I asked Jean-Luc what was wrong.
COLIN _____
2   He announced that he had had his first dream in English.
JEAN-LUC _____
3   I asked him to tell me about it.
COLIN _____
4   He said he couldn't tell me about it.
JEAN-LUC _____
5   He hadn't understood anything.
JEAN-LUC _____

J   Discussion

Gwen was reading *The Interpretation of Dreams* by Sigmund Freud.

Freud believed that by studying and analysing the dreams of his patients he could learn a lot about the problems and anxieties which had caused their illness.

However, it is not only people who are ill who have dreams. We all have dreams. What do you think causes them?

Do you believe, like Freud, that there is a deep significance to be found in our dreams?

Can you remember any of your own dreams? Talk about them.

Listening activity 🔘

K   Comprehension

Here are five statements referring to Professor Watkis's radio talk. Decide whether they are true or false:

1   He believed that normal people and people who were mentally ill were very different.
2   In the *Psychopathology of Everyday Life* Freud shows that many of the mistakes we make are not really accidents,
3   *The Psychopathology of Everyday Life* is concerned mainly with the behaviour of people who are mentally ill.
4   Freud believed that when we forget things it is usually because they are not really important to us.
5   It is quite difficult to get hold of a book containing accounts of Freud's original research.

L   Gap dictation

This unit is different from the earlier ones. You can practise all your skills. You will need to read and listen at the same time and remember the correct response for the question words. Here is an example:

<u>When</u> did Sigmund Freud publish a book about the behaviour of normal people?
<u>In</u> 1914.

Answer more questions.

1   What was Sigmund Freud doing when he developed his system of psychoanalysis?
    . . .
2   How did he find that illness could often be traced back to problems or conflicts?
    . . .
3   What else did he discover at this time?
    . . .
4   What conclusions did he reach?
    . . .
5   What did he demonstrate?
    . . .

M   Writing activity

The Psychopathology of Everyday Life explains why normal people sometimes behave strangely. Listen again to the extract from Professor Watkis's talk.

Make a short list of some of the things that normal people do which are strange.

N   Writing activity

In the United States, many comparatively normal people visit their 'analyst' more frequently than people in Europe go to see their dentist. They talk over their problems and he or she asks them about their dreams.

Write 250–350 words on dreams. You can write about your own dreams or about the subject generally.

Summary

In this unit we practise using 'should have' and 'shouldn't have'.

Examples:
The journey from London to Paris by train and boat was very slow and the train was very full. Annette said 'We *should have* come by air.'
Terry said: 'We *shouldn't have* travelled on a Saturday.'

John thought there was enough petrol in the tank to drive from Luton to London. In fact they ran out of petrol on the motorway.

What do you think John said?

We also practise the 'to have something done' construction.

Example:
I'm *going to have* this suit *cleaned.*
I *had* the car *serviced* last week.

What might you have done to a particularly good photograph you took?

Note also these useful phrasal verbs with 'pass' and 'give':
pass off, pass out, pass up, give away, give out, give off, give back, give up, give in.

Whart sort of things might cause somebody to pass out?

The soldiers raised a white flag. Explain why they did this. Use the verb 'give' + a preposition.

UNIT 18   The police at work

Reading activity

A CHELSEA DIARY

Here we are at the end of a week on the 10 pm to 6 am shift at Chelsea Police Station. It was a typical week.

Altogether we handled 183 incidents ranging from a lost dog to a nasty murder.

Here are a few highlights.

5.35 am Monday

PC Chris Jenkins saw a man trying to start a car parked next to the police station.

'Having trouble?' he asked.

The man nodded. Chris pointed out that he didn't have the key. 'No, I don't,' said the man. 'I know,' said Chris. 'It's my car. I'm arresting you.'

PC Chris Jenkins

6am Tuesday

The highest tide for centuries was running and a call came in that several of the house-boats moored at Cheyne Walk had broken loose.

Sergeant Watson

Sergeant Watson, the relief sergeant, grabbed 12 constables who were just going home and took them down to the river in the van.

They had a difficult time getting lines across to some of the sleepy householders. But, finally they secured all the houseboats and got soaking wet doing it.

It's OK now, though. They're on speaking terms with Sergeant Watson again.

1.15 am Wednesday

A publican who lives in a flat over his pub phoned. He had been awakened by the crash of breaking glass and was sure he was being burgled.

PC Eric Trimmer

We turned up in strength. The van with four of us in it got there a couple of seconds before the panda car.

There was no sign of a break-in, but we discovered an unconscious man on the floor of the pub bleeding all over the place. PC Eric Trimmer was able to stop the bleeding and save the man's life.

He'd fallen from the window of a flat above the publican's and crashed through the pub's reinforced glass roof.

11 pm Thursday

An attractive young lady took all her clothes off and put them in a washing machine in an all-night launderette.

PC Danny Pierce

The night supervisor, a very proper old gentleman, took exception to this and called us. Despite plenty of offers a mass turn-out was avoided. PC Danny Pierce went round and restored the peace.

10.45 pm Friday

We got a call from a man who wanted us to find his wife. He sounded terribly upset. So we went round to see him in the panda car. The flat was run-down and his four kids were whimpering in the bedroom. It seems he had a fight with his wife who ran out of the flat and disappeared. He wanted to go and look for her. We calmed him down and talked him into staying with his children. (We left Woman PC Margaret Carter to keep them company.)

WPC Margaret Carter

It wasn't easy, because he'd hit his wife and injured her. He was nearly beside himself with guilt. Then we started trying to trace his wife.

Meanwhile Inspector Hicks discussed the situation with the local Children's Department, and went round to the flat to see how things were going.

Inspector Hicks

The next morning the mother telephoned to ask how the children were, but wouldn't say where she was.

11 pm Saturday

A group of football supporters started mixing it with another group in a pub not far from the station. Everybody who was free went.

Nobody got hurt seriously. We had to arrest three of them who couldn't be quietened down. But it was fun while it lasted and they apologised for all the fuss the next morning.

Sunday

It was an appropriately quiet day. A couple of cars were stolen and turned up later.

A few minor thefts were investigated. The nicest thing that happened was finding the children's mother who'd disappeared on Friday.

We persuaded her to go back to her husband and family. Not strictly in the line of duty. But nobody likes to see children end up in care if it can be avoided.

All in all it wasn't an unusually exciting week. Not for Chelsea.

A   Questions

1 What was the man arrested by PC Jenkins on Monday intending to do?

2 What was the emergency that occurred on Tuesday?

3 Can you explain why the constables involved in the Tuesday incident weren't too pleased with Sgt Watson? Give two reasons.

4 When the publican was woken up in the early hours of Wednesday morning, what did he think was happening?

5 Why do you imagine the attractive young lady took her clothes off?

6 Why had the wife with four children left her husband?

7 Explain how the police became involved with the football supporters.

8 What did the policeman mean by 'It was fun while it lasted.'?

B   Vocabulary exercise

1 The writer mentions the 10 pm to 6.0 am *shift*. Can you think of any other people who work on shifts? Why is shift-work sometimes necessary?

2 Sgt Watson *grabbed* 12 constables. Why might somebody grab a friend's arm in a bus or train?

3 The publican was sure he was being *burgled*. How do burglars usually get into houses or flats?

4 When the young lady took off her clothes, a *mass turn-out* was avoided. Can you think of any situations where you would expect there to be a mass turn-out?

5 The kids were *whimpering* because their parents had quarrelled. Can you think of any animals that whimper? Why do they do this?

6 The man had *injured* his wife. Have you ever been injured? Explain how it happened.

7 Nobody got *hurt*. What would you do if you had a tooth that was hurting? Give an example of something that happened to you and hurt very much.

8 Sunday was an *appropriately* quiet day. Think of an appropriate present to be given to a policeman by his colleagues after 40 years service with the force.

C   Vocabulary exercise

There are quite a lot of idiomatic expressions in the Reading activity and your dictionary will not always give you much help. In this exercise, some of the idiomatic expressions are included. We advise you to study the Reading activity, notice how the original phrases are used and then choose the most accurate answers. There may be more than one correct answer.

1   Here are a few *highlights*.
   a specific topics
   b main points
   c interesting specimens
   d special topics

2   Chris *pointed out* that he didn't have a key.
   a explained
   b showed
   c indicated
   d demonstrated

3   They are *on speaking terms* with Sergeant Watson again.
   a They must speak to him again.
   b They don't mind speaking to him again.
   c They are allowed to speak to him again.
   d They are willing to speak to him again.

4   The night supervisor, a very proper old man, *took exception to* this, and called us.
   a disagreed with
   b disapproved of
   c refused to
   d objected to

5   The flat was *run down* and his four kids were whimpering in the bedroom.
   a not fit
   b not healthy
   c not well
   d not looked-after

6   A group of football supporters started *mixing it* with another group in a pub not far from the station.
   a arguing
   b disturbing
   c fighting
   d insulting

7   Everybody who was *free* went.
   a not on holiday
   b not on duty
   c not expensive
   d not occupied

8   They apologised for all the *fuss* the next morning.
   a attention
   b worry
   c trouble
   d disturbance

9   *All in all*, it wasn't an unusually exciting week. Not for Chelsea.
   a Considering everything
   b Estimating everything
   c Adding everything
   d Thinking about everything

D   Discussion

In Britain, policemen have to be at least 5 feet 8 inches (172 cm) tall. They also have to be fit and strong.

What qualities does a good police constable require?

What problems might a police constable have to deal with during an eight-hour shift from 6.0 am to 2.0 pm?

E   Practice activity

When the police arrived at the pub, they found an injured man lying on the floor. PC Trimmer told the Inspector later that he had been able to stop the bleeding.
PC Trimmer said: 'I was able to stop the bleeding.'

What were the exact words used by each speaker?

1   PC Jenkins asked the man why he'd tried to steal his car.
   PC Jenkins said: _____
2   Sgt Watson told the 12 constables who were just going off duty that they were needed at Cheyne Walk.
   He said: _____
3   Later Sgt Watson thanked the constables and told them they could go and have their breakfast.
   He said: _____
4   PC Danny Pierce asked the young lady why she'd taken her clothes off.
   He said: _____
5   Woman PC Margaret Carter said she would stay with the children for a while.
   She said: _____

6 One of the football supporters told the police that the other group had started the trouble.
He said: _____

7 The children's mother agreed to go home.
She said: _____

8 One of the policemen said they always disliked seeing children end up in care.
He said: _____

F Practice activity

The police eventually persuaded the children's mother to return home to her husband and children. One of the policemen probably said something like this:

'Don't you think you should go back home? I really think you ought to go back home.'

Practise persuading people to do things:

1 A friend has had her purse stolen. She doesn't want to report the theft to the police . . .

2 A friend has been complaining of mysterious headaches for some time, but hasn't seen a doctor . . .

3 A friend stayed at your home overnight after a party and doesn't feel like going to work this morning. If he or she doesn't go, there'll be trouble . . .

When we want to persuade someone *not* to do something, we can say:

'I (really) don't think you should (ought to) send that letter.'

Now practise persuading people *not* to do things:

4 A friend says he is going to ask his boss for a pay rise. You don't think this is wise at the moment . . .

5 A friend has quarrelled with his or her family and has threatened to leave home. You don't think this is a good idea . . .

6 A friend tells you he is fed up with his job and has decided to hand in his notice. But it won't be easy to get another job . . .

G Practice activity

If you wish to ask somebody to do something, the polite way is to say:
'Would you please . . . ?'

or if you are speaking to a stranger you might say:
'I wonder if you could possibly . . . ?'

Practise asking people to do things.

1 How might a sister in a hospital tell a nurse to go to the operating theatre immediately?

2 How might you ask a stranger to change a bank-note?

3 How might a police constable ask a police sergeant to move his car?

4 How might the manager of a shop tell one of his staff, who is going to post a parcel, to bring back a receipt?

5 You take some negatives to be printed and you want the prints as soon as possible. What might you say to the assistant?

6 How might a teacher inform a class that he wants the homework handed in the next day?

Dialogue 📼

It is Sunday morning at Chelsea Police Station. WPC Margaret Carter has just gone into an interview room with Carol Townsend. Read the Impression questions before you listen to their conversation.

H Impression questions

1 Listening to the sounds, what do you think is going on at the Police Station?

2 Why do you think WPC Carter took Carol Townsend to a private interview room?

3 How would you describe the way Carol was feeling?

4 Carol said: 'They could have told me.' Who do you think she meant?

5 How do you think Carol is feeling about her husband?

6 Carol said: 'I don't believe you' to Margaret Carter. That sounds rude, but what do you think she really wanted to say?

7 Why do you think WPC Carter spent some time with Carol's children?

8 How do you feel about the WPC's attitude to Carol? For example, do you feel she is sympathetic?

The police at work

9 WPC Carter said: 'As long as you both want me to.' What do you think she meant?

10 In your opinion, what should Carol Townsend say to her husband? What do you think he should say to her?

I Focus questions

In this interview, there were a lot of examples of stress on particular words, probably because Carol was upset and emotional.

Listen to the interview again and underline the stressed words you hear.
1 They miss you.
2 Why don't you just see him?
3 Why should I?
4 All right then. I do want to see them.
5 Them yes, but if he's there . . .

WPC Carter managed to persuade Carol Townsend to see her husband. She used language to help her. These are some of the things she said. Say what she was trying to do with the language.

Example:
Like a cup of coffee, Mrs Townsend?
She was inviting Mrs Townsend to have a cup of coffee, but she was also calming her down.

You continue.

1 They miss you. Wouldn't you like to see them?
2 Don't you think you should try to make things up?
3 Talk things over.
4 I'll get him to come here if you like.
5 As long as you both want me to.

Listening activity 👓

J Comprehension

Here are eight statements referring to the interview. Decide whether they are true or false:

1 PC Parker usually travels around in a police car.
2 A Home-Beat Officer isn't concerned with catching criminals.
3 PC Parker is interested in the families of troublemakers.
4 People don't normally mind being asked questions by the Home-Beat Officer.
5 PC Parker never annoys people.
6 PC Parker sometimes has to deal with personal injuries.
7 One of the things PC Parker likes about his job is the element of uncertainty about what the day will bring.
8 PC Parker believes that the people who live in his area like to see him there.

K Gap dictation

In the Listening activity, there are groups of words that we associate together. Listen again and write these groups of words.

MARJORIE HENDERSON Now, (1)____ ____ ____ ____ listeners, can you explain exactly what a Home-Beat Officer is? (2)____ is he (3)____ ____ the policemen who go tearing round in big white cars?

PETER PARKER Well, the Home-Beat Officer (4)____ ____ ____ a comparatively small area and (5)____ ____ ____ to get to know that area and everybody who lives there, (6)____ ____ ____ ____ ____ ____.

MARJORIE HENDERSON So he (7)____ ____ ____ ____ ____ all the criminals who live in his area?

PETER PARKER Yes, if there *are* any criminals on his patch (8)____ ____ ____ ____, but he's concerned (9)____ ____ ____ crime prevention (10)____ ____ ____ ____ catching criminals.

MARJORIE HENDERSON And of course he (11)____ ____ ____ all the teenagers and potentail troublemakers.

127

L   Writing activity

Listen to the interview again. Can you make a short summary of the duties of the Home-Beat Officer?

M   Writing activity

Is a police force necessary?

Discuss this question. Then write about 250 words.

Summary

In this unit we practise turning reported speech into direct speech.

Examples:
He asked why I hadn't telephoned at once.
He said: 'Why didn't you telephone at once?'
Margaret offered to pay for the taxi.
She said: 'I'll pay for the taxi.'

George apologised for breaking my binoculars and said he would have them repaired. What were George's actual words?

We also practise persuading people to do or not to do things.

Examples:
I really think you ought to telephone him and explain.

Don't you think you ought to telephone him and explain?
I don't think you ought to go and see him.

How would you persuade a friend who wants to walk home late at night to let you ring for a taxi?

We also practise asking people to do things:
Example:
Would you please take this note to Dr Jeffries at once and wait for a reply?

What might an au pair say to a little boy who doesn't want to go to bed?

UNIT 19 Love and marriage

Reading activity

EDWARD AND MRS SIMPSON

1 Choosing the right husband or wife is never an easy business, but it is even
more difficult if you are the heir to a great throne.

When George V, the King of England, died in December 1936, his eldest son,
Edward, the handsome and popular Prince of Wales, became King and the
5 coronation was planned for the following May. Edward was still unmarried.
Some years before, however, he had met an American lady, of whom he had
become very fond. Her name was Wallis Simpson. She was divorced and had
then married an English shipping broker. Other princes have been known to
have discreet friendships with ladies and for a considerable time no mention of
10 the matter was made in the English press. But many stories appeared in
foreign papers, particularly when Mrs Simpson brought a divorce action
against her husband. The following announcement was published in the *New
York Journal* of October 26, 1936:

> Within a few days Mrs Ernest Simpson . . . will obtain her divorce decree in
> England, and some eight months thereafter she will be married to Edward
> VIII, King of England . . . He (Edward) believes . . . that it would be an actual
> mistake for a King of England to marry into any of the royal houses of the
> continent of Europe, and so involve himself and his Empire in the
> complications and disasters of these royal houses. He believes, further, that in
> this day and generation it is absurd to maintain the tradition of royal inter-
> marriages, with all the physical as well as the political disabilities likely to
> result from that outgrown custom . . .
> . . . Primarily, however, the King's transcendent reason for marrying Mrs
> Simpson is that he ardently loves her, and does not see why a King should be
> denied the privilege of marrying the lady he loves.

It must be appreciated that in Britain the sovereign is head of the Church of
15 England, and the Church of England does not allow the re-marriage of
divorced persons. Whatever the King may have thought, there were those in
high places who saw his intended marriage to Mrs Simpson as a dreadful
threat to the monarchy. The Prime Minister came to see the King and
requested him to persuade Mrs Simpson to withdraw her divorce petition.
20 The King refused.

It is interesting to speculate about what might have happened had the British
had the custom of holding a referendum on important matters, as is common
in some countries, for Edward was tremendously popular with the ordinary
people. At all events, the story broke very suddenly. People were stunned and
25 bewildered. Hard and perhaps unfair things were written about Mrs Simpson
in the English papers. Stones were thrown at the windows of her house in
Cumberland Terrace and she hurriedly left the country.

'I believe I know what the people would tolerate and what they would not,'
the Prime Minister told the King, meaning that the people would not accept
30 Mrs Simpson as the Queen. The King replied that he intended to marry Mrs
Simpson and was prepared to go.

On 10 December, the King formally abdicated. He made a farewell speech to
the people on the radio and sailed away in a destroyer to Boulogne and
travelled to Austria to stay with friends. When Wallis Simpson's divorce
35 became absolute, she and Edward were married.

In May of 1937 the coronation took place, as planned, with one major change
in the arrangements. It was Edward's younger brother, George, who was
crowned. George VI reigned until 1952, when he was succeeded by his
daughter, Queen Elizabeth II.

A   Questions

1 What rank did Edward hold in 1935?
2 Why do you think it was some time before any mention was made in English newspapers of Edward's friendship with Mrs Simpson?
3 What were the arguments put forward by the writer in the *New York Journal* in favour of Edward's marrying Wallis Simpson?
4 Can you explain why the Prime Minister asked the King to persuade Mrs Simpson to withdraw her divorce petition?
5 What might have happened had the Government held a referendum?
6 What is the relationship between Edward and Queen Elizabeth II?

B   Vocabulary exercise

1 *Choosing* the right husband or wife is difficult. When did you last have to make a choice?
2 Edward became *fond of* Wallis. What sort of things are you fond of?
3 The American journalist writes of 'the complications and *disasters* of these royal houses.' Can you think of some famous disasters not connected with royalty?
4 The writer continues: 'It is *absurd* to maintain the tradition.' Have you heard of anything recently that you consider absurd?
5 '. . . he does not see why the King should be denied the *privilege* of marrying the lady he loves'. If I joined a sports club, what privileges do you think I might enjoy?
6 There were those who saw the marriage as a dreadful *threat* to the monarchy. What forms of action might a trade union threaten to take? Why would they do this?
7 To *speculate* is to consider and perhaps discuss. What sort of things do gossip columnists in newspapers speculate about?

8 People were *stunned* and *bewildered*. How might a goalkeeper in a football match be stunned? When did you last feel 'completely bewildered'?

C   Vocabulary exercise

Here are ten excerpts from the Reading activity. Without looking at the text, find the prepositions that could be used to complete each excerpt

Other princes have been known to have discreet friendships (1)_____ ladies and (2)_____ a considerable time no mention (3)_____ the matter was made in the British press.

But many stories appeared (4)_____ foreign papers, particularly when Mrs Simpson brought a divorce action (5)_____ her husband.

'(6)_____ a few days, Mrs Ernest Simpson will obtain her divorce decree (7)_____ England and some eight months thereafter she will be married (8)_____ Edward VIII, King of England.'

He believes that it would be an actual mistake (9)_____ a King of England to marry into any of the royal houses of the continent of Europe and so involve himself and his Empire (10)_____ the complications and disasters of these royal houses.

D   Discussion

Think about the problems of choosing a marriage partner. It must be particularly difficult for princes and princesses.

But what about ordinary people? Do you think it is a good thing if the boy and girl have similar characters – or is it better if they are 'opposites'?

What about the age of the two people concerned? At what age should people get married? Should they both be the same age?

Should they have similar tastes?

Do you think marrying a foreigner might cause special problems? In what way?

E   Writing activity

Note this sentence from the Reading activity:

It is interesting to speculate about what might have happened, *had the British had the custom* of holding a referendum ... (line 21)

The same idea might be expressed less dramatically like this:
It is interesting to speculate about what might have happened, if the British had had the custom of holding a referendum ...

The form 'Had it/had it not ... , ... would have/wouldn't have ... ' is used more frequently in written than in spoken English.

Study these ideas:
It rained/the football match was cancelled.
Had it not rained, the football match wouldn't have been cancelled.
The President was assassinated/there was a war.
Had the President not been assassinated, there wouldn't have been a war.

Match up the statements in the left-hand column with those in the right-hand column and make eight sentences beginning with 'Had ... '
Use each statement once only.

They went on strike.	He was killed.
She was the best actress available.	They lost their jobs.
The International Red Cross brought in supplies of food.	He was sent to prison.
	She got the part.
She wrote the novel.	He was employed by Ferrari.
She drove through the red traffic-light.	She became famous.
He stole the money.	She was stopped by the police.
He joined the army.	Many of the peasants survived.
He was a first-class driver.	

F   Practice activity

Glen Harris was an American radio commentator at the time of the abdication of King Edward. He considered that the British 'Establishment' were being very unfair to the King. This is what he said:

'According to British law, the woman who the King marries will automatically become the Queen. But it is impossible for Mrs Simpson to be crowned Queen, owing to the fact that she has been through the divorce courts.

Of course, Parliament always has the power to change the law if it seems necessary or desirable. In this case, however, the Prime Minister has announced that the Government have no intention of changing the law. In other words, they are determined to force the King to choose between Mrs Simpson and his throne.

Clearly, the King is deeply in love with Mrs Simpson and I believe a king has the same right as any other man to marry the woman he loves. The British Government should change the law immediately so that the King may marry Mrs Simpson and retain his rightful position as King.'

Imagine you are a newspaper reporter who heard Glen Harris. Write a report of what he said for your newspaper. We have begun each paragraph: Speaking on New York radio last night Glen Harris said that according to British law, the woman whom the King married . . .

He added that Parliament always had . . .

He argued that the King . . .

G   Practice activity

Note this extract from the text:
In May of 1937, the Coronation *took place* as planned . . . (line 36)

The verb 'take' is frequently used with prepositions and adverbs. For example:

You'd better *take off* your shoes.

Do you know what time our plane *takes off?*

When John was promoted, his salary went up, but naturally he had to *take on* a lot more responsibility.

Haagenson didn't *take up* tennis till he was 24, and here he is in the final of the tournament.

Some babies *take after* their fathers, some take after their mothers and some don't seem to take after anybody.

Poor Mrs Prendergast was completely *taken in* by the young man's story.

The policeman *took down* the number of the car.

When Henderson was sacked, Fox *took over* the job of sales manager.

I'll *take care of* your suitcase while you get a cup of tea.

Certainly I borrowed Roger's typewriter, but I *took it back* that evening.

Replace the words in italics by suitable expressions with 'take'. Use each expression once only:

1 My aunt agreed to *look after* the children while we were on holiday.
2 When the sales manager retired, George agreed to *do* the extra work.
3 Tony has a terrible temper. He obviously *gets it from* his mother.
4 I want to lose a bit of weight so everyone tells me I should eat less and *start* jogging.
5 I think you'd better *make a note* of this telephone number.
6 The young woman certainly looked innocent, but I wasn't *fooled* for a moment by her account of how she got the jewellery.

Dialogue 📼

Peter and Moira have been married for two years. It is ten past six now and they've been watching the news on television. A leading story was the visit by the Prince and Princess of Wales to a new factory in Cardiff.

After you have listened to their conversation, answer the Impression questions. If you need to listen again, ask your teacher.

H   Impression questions

1 Why do you think Peter and Moira switched off the TV?
2 Peter didn't finish his sentence: 'No more worries about bills, mortgages . . .' What words do you think could finish it?
3 Moira said that Peter would have plenty of other worries if he were a prince. What do you think these worries might be?
4 Do you think Moira sympathised with the problems of the Prince and Princess? How do you know?
5 How do you think Peter felt about them?
6 What, in your opinion, is the difference between 'a job' and 'a way of life'?
7 How was Peter feeling when he said, 'There you are.'
8 What do you think Peter was referring to when he said 'That's one problem they haven't got.'

Love and marriage

UNIT 19

I   Focus questions

We often use sounds rather than words to tell people what we think or how we feel. Listen to this example.

Now listen to Peter and Moira in another conversation. Write the words you think could replace the sounds you hear.

1   MOIRA   Did you enjoy your apple tart, Peter?
     PETER

2   MOIRA   And what did you think of the new cheese?
     PETER

3   PETER   By the way, Moira, I've got to work this weekend.
     MOIRA

4   PETER   Another thing. I'll have to get up at five tomorrow.
     MOIRA

5   PETER   But I haven't forgotten your birthday. Would you like to open your present?
     MOIRA

Listening activity 📼

J   Comprehension

Here are eight statements referring to the interview. Decide whether they are true or false:

1   A Hollywood producer sees marriage as an unromantic business.
2   In some countries, young people who are going to be married do not see one another until the day of the wedding.
3   In Japan, when an arranged marriage takes place, the bride and bridegroom have previously met one another and talked.
4   Professor Stuart suggests that in Africa women do not make important decisions.
5   He also suggests that having several wives is an excellent arrangement as far as the men are concerned.
6   Professor Stuart thinks that people who get married are not necessarily taking a risk.
7   American women who married African men have generally been disappointed with their marriage.
8   Professor Stuart believes that an arranged marriage is more likely to produce a happy marriage than the Western system.

An English wedding

An Indian wedding

133

K   Gap dictation

Before you listen again to a part of Professor Stuart's radio talk, have a good look at the Gap dictation. Try to imagine what the missing words are and think about how they should be spelt. Spelling is important in this exercise. To help you, we have a given a space for each letter of the words.

In Japan, (1)_____, arranged marriages still take place. But there things (2)_____ _____ in a different way. A girl (3)_____ _____ _____ a husband and the girl's mother, or aunt perhaps, (4)_____ the mother of a (5)_____ young man and the young (6)_____ are (7)_____. They (8)_____ _____ _____ to have a look at one another and if one (9)_____ _____ says, 'Oh, no. I could never marry him or her,' they (10)_____ _____ _____ _____ _____.

Now listen, fill in the gaps and check your ideas about the missing words.

L   Writing activity

Professor Stuart talks about marriage in India, Japan, Africa and Europe.

Can you summarise briefly what he has to say about each kind of marriage?

M   Writing activity

In some countries arranged marriages are quite common.

What are the advantages and disadvantages?

Write about 250 words.

Summary

In this unit we practise using inverted conditionals beginning with 'had'.

Example:
Had I realised how late it was, I would certainly have taken a taxi.

Express the same idea using 'if'.

We also practise turning a longer passage of direct speech into reported speech.

Examples:
MR SCOTT   'The members of our union are very angry.'
Mr Scott said (that) the members of his union were very angry.
MR SCOTT   'They have not been so angry for many years.'
Mr Scott said (that) they had not been so angry for many years.

MR SCOTT   'If it is necessary we shall call upon our members to strike.'
Mr Scott said (that) if it was necessary they would call upon their members to strike.

Mr Scott then said he regretted any inconvenience the dispute might cause to members of the public, but added that he felt sure they would understand that it was up to the union to safeguard the interests of its members.

What were Mr Scott's actual words?

Note also these useful phrasal verbs with 'take': take off, take on, take up, take after, take in, take down, take over, take back.

Have you taken up any new hobbies recently? What?
Do you think you take after your mother or your father?

UNIT 20   Ireland

Reading activity

THE POLITICAL SITUATION IN IRELAND

1   There are many odd corners of the earth where accidents of history have led to violent conflict between different sections of the community. But nowhere perhaps has any government been presented with a more intractable problem than that of Northern Ireland.

5   The problem stems from a most unfortunate decision taken by a seventeenth-century British government to encourage Protestants from Scotland to emigrate to Catholic Ireland.

Political differences can cause problems, religious disagreements can present difficulties, but when religious differences and political differences become
10   interlocked, the confusion that follows presents problems so complex that they become well-nigh impossible to solve.

The south of Ireland is a republic with a mainly Catholic population. The north remains part of the United Kingdom. The population of the north is part Catholic and part Protestant, with the Protestants in the majority. For
15   many years the Protestants ruled in Northern Ireland and the opportunities for a Catholic were limited. The Protestant always seemed to get the top job.

Eventually, trouble flared up and the British Government sent in British

troops to keep the peace between the two sections of the community. At first the soldiers were welcomed, but gradually the feelings of the Catholic
20   community have changed to irritation, to dislike and sometimes to hatred.

The IRA is a Catholic military force, dedicated to 'throwing the British troops out of Ireland'. They would also like to see Northern Ireland become part of a united Ireland. The IRA see themselves as gallant freedom fighters. The British Government and the vast majority of the British people regard them as
25   terrorists.

Were a referendum to be held tommorow, it is conceivable that the British would vote in favour of withdrawing the troops from Ireland. Many Britishers would be quite happy to see the North united with the South. But this is a prospect which would horrify the Protestant majority in the North. They
30   would be appalled at the thought of suddenly finding themselves a Protestant minority in a united Catholic Ireland.

So where does any British government go from here? Political assassinations continue. British soldiers are shot. A few days ago I was discussing Ireland with an Irishman, a Catholic from the south. 'I can tell you this,' he said, 'no
35   English government will ever solve the Irish problem, because there isn't an Englishman capable of understanding it.'

I wonder if my Irish friend is right.

A   Questions

1   If an Irishman said: 'The trouble in the north is all the fault of the British Government,' what moment in history is he probably thinking of?
2   Could we describe Ireland as a Kingdom? Give your reasons.
3   Why did the British Government send soldiers to Ireland?
4   What is the IRA?
5   How do you think a bank manager living in the south of England might regard the IRA?
6   How do you think a bank employee working in Dublin might regard the IRA?
7   How do you think the same bank employee working in Dublin might feel about the prospect of the North of Ireland joining the South?
8   How do you think a Protestant living in Belfast would feel about it? Why?
9   How do you think an English bus driver living in London might feel about the unification of Ireland?
10   Why do you think the Irishman said: 'No English government will ever solve the Irish problem . . . ' (line 34)

B   Vocabulary exercise

1   Northern Ireland presents the Government with an *intractable problem.* (line 3) Can you think of any other intractable problems of a similar nature in other parts of the world?
2   The problem *stems from* a decision taken by a seventeenth-century British government. (line 5) What might the defeat of a football team stem from? What might the fall of a government stem from?
3   Can you think of any countries to which large numbers of people have *emigrated* over the last 100 years?
4   Can you think of any region where political trouble has *flared* up recently?
5   What sort of things would you expect *terrorists* to do?
6   What sort of issues might be decided by having a *referendum?*
7   Can you think of any item of news which you might hear on the radio that would *horrify* you?
8   Can you think of any *assassinations* which have taken place during recent years? What about assassination attempts that failed?

C   Vocabulary exercise

As you know, it is very common in English to use prefixes to change the meaning of words. The Reading activity used the expressions 'an unfortunate decision' and 'impossible problems'. 'Un-', 'im-', and 'in-' are negative prefixes. Use one of these three prefixes to disagree with the following statements. Here is an example taken from the Reading activity.

a Many Britishers would be quite *happy* to see the North united with the South.
b I'm afraid I disagree. They would be quite *unhappy*.

1a   It is conceivable that the British would vote in favour of withdrawing the troops from Ireland.
b   No, it isn't. It's absolutely _____

2a   Most Englishmen are capable of understanding the Irish problem.
b   I disagree. In my opinion they are completely _____

3a   At first, the British troops were made welcome.
b   That may be, but at the moment they are very _____

4a   I think it is probable that an agreement will soon be reached.
b   Do you really? I think it is most _____.

5a   Surely their behaviour is excusable in such circumstances.
b   Not at all. It is quite _____.

6a   Wouldn't you agree that it is natural to be patriotic?
b   Yes, but it is _____ to be a fanatic.

7a   In my opinion people are usually moderate.
b   Do you really think so? I think people are often _____.

8a   I feel that a referendum would be desirable.
b   Well, I don't. I think it would be _____.

9a   Don't you think my arguments have been reasonable?
b   No, I don't. They've been totally _____.

10a   What about the facts. Aren't they accurate?
b   I'm afraid not. I find them all _____.

D   Discussion

It is difficult to discuss Northern Ireland and what should be done there, without knowing quite a lot about the situation.

What do you think about the trouble?

Are there any other parts of the world where there are similar problems?

How do you feel about South Africa and apartheid, for instance?

If you worked for the United Nations, what recommendations would you make to the British Government?

Are there any recommendations you would like to make to the Government of the Republic of Ireland?

E   Practice activity

In any situation where there is a security problem, innocent people are often questioned and searched by soldiers and policemen. In such situations it is usually not a good idea to object or refuse.

In ordinary circumstances, however, being able to refuse to do something firmly or politely is often useful. When you refuse politely, you often add an excuse.

Example (a)   Move your car immediately. Certainly not. I got here first.

Example (b)   Will you move that car, please? I'm afraid I can't just at the moment. It won't start.

Example (a)   is a firm refusal, made in reply to an aggressive instruction by someone in no special position of authority.

Example (b)   is a polite refusal.

Practise refusing to do things. Decide whether you wish to be 'firm' or 'polite'. Imagine you are a guest staying at a hotel.

1   You're in the television room watching a football match. Another guest comes in and says rudely: 'Turn over to the other channel at once.'
2   There is a disco at the hotel and another guest you don't like at all asks you to dance.

3   You've been playing tennis for about 15 minutes when two other guests who want to play arrive and say: 'Come on, it's time you finished your game.'

4   Another guest invites you to go for a drive in his or her car. You don't want to go.

5   Another guest you dont really like says: 'Ah, you've got a tennis racquet, haven't you? Can I borrow it for the afternoon?'

6   An elderly lady says: 'I wonder if you could possibly give me a lift to the station in your car?' You have a car, but you will be busy all afternoon.

F   Practice activity

Expressing one's opinion about sensitive issues is difficult enough in one's own language. In a language other than one's own it is very difficult indeed. However, you will find the phrases in italics useful:

I believe it was foolish to encourage Protestants to emigrate to Ireland.

In my opinion it was the wrong decision.

I'm inclined to think it was done for monetary gain.

Which of the expressions above might help you to turn these statements into opinions expressed with more diplomacy and accuracy?

1   It's an impossible book to read.
2   That man should never have been promoted.
3   He's the most talented writer writing today.
4   Books should never be turned into films.
5   Modern pop music is rubbish.

Now choose some recent event – it might be a court case that has caused a lot of interest – it might be an exciting football match.

Divide into groups of three or four and discuss it, practising the use of the expressions above.

G   Practice activity

Study these new phrasal verbs:

As soon as the policeman arrived, the youths *cleared off*.

Mr Salt's disappearance is a mystery that has never been *cleared up*.

'Oh, did I tell you? Molly *dropped in* yesterday.'

Eventually the sound of the engine *died away* in the distance.

Last time he *let us down* by not turning up.

He was found guilty of driving while under the influence of alcohol, but the judge *let him off* with a fine.

I hope you've *settled down* in your new home.

'Look, I don't have any money at the moment. Can I *settle up* with you tomorrow?'

He's my friend and I shall *stand by* him, whatever he's done.

'Harry certainly *slipped up* when he offered blackmarket tickets to that policeman.'

Replace the words in italics by suitable phrasal verbs from those illustrated above. Use each verb once only:

1   I'm afraid we *made a mistake* when we quoted £100 for that job. It should have been at least £200.
2   When Mr Wood saw the little boys playing near his new car, he was very worried. '*Go away* at once,' he said.
3   Even though Binns was sent to prison, his wife *remained loyal to* him.
4   'Have you seen Joe recently?'
    'Yes, he *called in* last week.'
5   'Did you remember to pay the bill for the repairs to the car?'
    'Yes, I *paid* yesterday.'
6   'Who's going to provide the music for the party?'
    'Fred's promised to see to that. He's very reliable. He won't *disappoint* us.'
7   The sound of the brass band *faded*, the procession disappeared from view and Paul was left standing alone beneath the poplar trees.
8   He was stopped for speeding and taken to court. But the magistrate *didn't punish him*.

Dialogue 🔊

Eric Johnson and his wife, Kathy, live in Devon, in a peaceful and picturesque village. Eric has just returned home after a day at work. Study these Impression questions. After you have thought about them, listen to the conversation.

H Impression questions

1 How do you think Eric felt when he got home from work?
2 What do you think he did when he got home from work?
3 What was Kathy doing?
4 How do you think Kathy knew that the news wasn't good?
5 What did Kathy mean when she said, 'I don't know.'
6 Eric asked a question and then answered it himself. Why do you think he did that?
7 Kathy said, 'It can't be much fun . . . '. What do you think she was trying to say?
8 How did Kathy change the conversation?
9 What was the point she was trying to make?
10 Why do you think Eric decided that it was time for tea?

Listen to the conversation now.

I Focus questions

A variety of attitudes were expressed in the Dialogue. Find at least one example of these attitudes and make a note. Listen again.

1 Interest
2 Suggestion
3 Despair
4 Sympathy
5 Accusation

J Discussion

Violence seems to be on the increase in so many places. Why do you think this is?

In Britain, murderers may be given long prison sentences, but there is no capital punishment. Yet policemen in Britain do not normally carry guns. What are your views on this?

Do you think that the re-introduction of capital punishment would help in reducing the number of violent crimes?

Listening activity 🔊

K   Comprehension

Here are eight statements referring to the advertisement. Decide whether they are true or false:

1   This advertisement is designed to encourage people to spend holidays in Ireland and take their cars with them.
2   The cars are unloaded from the plane at Dublin Airport, Cork Airport, or Shannon Airport.
3   Some of the people who go on these holidays hire cars when they get to Ireland.
4   If you go on one of these holidays you will have the chance to ride a horse.
5   You will also have the chance to visit the seaside.
6   Dublin is the capital of Northern Ireland.
7   Dublin has kept its own identity.
8   A number of well-known writers have lived in Dublin.

Ireland

UNIT 20

L   Gap dictation

Before you listen again to part of the advertisement, study the Gap dictation exercise and try to imagine what the missing words are. You will be expected to spell the missing words correctly. To help you, we have left a space for each letter of the missing words.

A return (1)_____ to Ireland, a self-drive car with (2)_____ free (3)_____ and Ireland's open roads, all at a (4)_____ _____ price. That's the (5)_____ and good (6)_____ of the Freeway motoring plan. Fly from (7)_____ of (8)_____ airports to Dublin, or into the (9)_____ of Ireland's (10)_____ at Cork or Shannon. It only takes about (11)_____ and then you're out on the (12)_____ _____, fresh and (13)_____, with a (14)_____ holiday ahead.

Now listen and write the missing words. Of course you will have the opportunity of listening again to check what you have written after you have finished.

M   Writing activity

Listen to the advertisement again. Make a list of the things you could do on an Irish holiday.

N   Writing activity

Look at the map of Ireland and the illustrations. Imagine that you have decided to spend a holiday in Ireland.
Write to a friend in the USA who does not speak your mother tongue telling him or her about your plans, where you intend to go and what you intend to do.

Summary

In this unit we practise refusing to do things firmly or politely.

Examples:
You and a friend are sitting in the television room at a hotel, watching a football match. Another guest comes in and says rather rudely:
'Turn over to the other channel. I want to watch the news.'

You could say: 'Certainly not. We got here first.'

Or if you wanted to be more polite:
'I'm afraid we're watching the football match.'

What do you think *you* might say in these circumstances? And what do you think might affect the manner of your reply?

We also practise expressing opinions about sensitive issues. (See Practice activity F.)

Here are two remarks about a film:
'There was too much violence.'
'It was too long.'

Can you express these ideas in a more diplomatic way?

Note also these useful phrasal verbs:
clear off, clear up, drop in, die away, let down, let off, settle down, settle up, stand by, slip up, wear out.

How might a member of a football team let down his team-mates?

If your friend had an overcoat that was worn out, what would you expect him to do?

141